OSPREY AIRCRAFT OF THE ACES • 7

Mustang Aces of the Ninth & Fifteenth Air Forces & the RAF

SERIES EDITOR: TONY HOLMES

OSPREY AIRCRAFT OF THE ACES • 7

Mustang Aces of the Ninth & Fifteenth Air Forces & the RAF

Jerry Scutts

OSPREY
AEROSPACE

First published in Great Britain in 1995 by Osprey Publishing
Elms Court, Chapel Way, Botley, Oxford, OX2 9LP

Reprinted Summer 1996, Summer 1999, 2004, 2005

ISBN 1 85532583 7

Edited by Tony Holmes
Design by TT Designs, Tony & Stuart Truscott

Cover Artwork by Iain Wyllie
Aircraft Profiles by Chris Davey, Keith Fretwell,
Mark Rolfe, Robert Simms and John Weal
Figure Artwork by Mike Chappell
Scale Drawings by Arthur Bentley
Chapter 5 and Appendices text by Jon Lake

Printed in Hong Kong

EDITOR'S NOTE
To make this best-selling series as authoritative as possible, the Editor would be
interested in hearing from any individual who may have relevant photographs,
documentation or first-hand experiences relating to the elite fighter pilots, and
their aircraft, of the various theatres of war. Any material used will be credited
to its original source. Please write to Tony Holmes at 16 Sandilands, Chipstead,
Sevenoaks, Kents, TN13 2SP, Great Britain, or by e-mail at:
tony.holmes@osprey-jets.freeserve.co.uk

Front cover
**Texan Col Charles M 'Sandy"
McCorkle turns his personalised
P-51B, Betty Jane, in towards a pair
of Ju 88s attempting to stem the
Allied push up through Italy in June
1944. Already a Spitfire Mk VIII ace
with the 31st FG, the 'scrappy'
McCorkle went on to claim another
six kills whilst flying Mustangs with
the Fifteenth AAF**

FOR A CATALOGUE OF ALL BOOKS PUBLISHED BY OSPREY MILITARY AND
AVIATION PLEASE CONTACT:

The Marketing Manager, Osprey Direct UK, PO Box 140,
Wellingborough, Northants, NN8 2FA, UK
Email: info@ospreydirect.co.uk

The Marketing Manager, Osprey Direct USA, c/o MBI Publishing,
PO Box 1, 729 Prospect Avenue, Osceola, WI 54020, USA.
Email: info@ospreydirectusa.com

www.ospreypublishing.com

CONTENTS

TACTICAL RECON

Following the first flight of the prototype North American NA-73X on 26 October 1940, the fighter ordered by the British Purchasing Commission (BPC) earlier that year took tangible form when mass-production began far away from the European war zone at Inglewood, California. With the threat of a German invasion postponed following the bitter fighting of the Battle of Britain, the BPC's efforts brought forth new types with which to strengthen the RAF for the coming offensive. Numerous existing and new American designs were ordered, with the NA-73 (soon to be christened the Mustang) being firmly in the latter category.

By the time the first Mustang Mk I (AG346) reached Britain for testing in October 1941, frontline RAF fighter squadrons were almost entirely equipped with the Supermarine Spitfire Mk V. This excellent fighter was in full production, and few airframe shortages were envisaged, a fact that made for great advantages in maintenance, repair

and supply of replacement machines. And as long as the Spitfire remained on a par with the leading Luftwaffe types, it made little sense to introduce a new fighter, particularly one reliant on the still-dangerous North Atlantic crossing for replacements and spares.

While the Mustang Mk I (powered by the Allison V-1710 engine) was one of the best US types delivered for RAF service due to its strong, 'quality', construction and good flying characteristics, it was no high altitude performer as it lacked a supercharger. Indeed, the aircraft could be quite a handful above 25,000 ft, but it was faster than the Spitfire Mk V, very manoeuvrable and most importantly, could remain aloft for four hours, giving it almost twice the endurance of the British fighter. Eight machine guns – six in the wings and two set alongside the engine crankcase – was a more than adequate armament.

Consequently, the Mustang Mk I initially found a niche in the RAF Order of Battle by undertaking a role previously handled by far less able types – namely that of Army co-operation. Created in December 1940, Army Co-operation Command's (ACC) brief was to 'organise, experiment and train in all forms of land-air co-operation'. One bitter lesson from the Battle of France had been a chronic lack of fast, well armed fighter-bombers to provide the Army not only with ground support through actual attack, but also timely photographic coverage of enemy dispositions. Such aircraft had, ideally, to possess the capability to fight their way out of situations where the enemy reacted vigorously. The Mustang, compared with the ACC's Lysanders and Tomahawks, seemed the ideal aircraft.

Inglewood, California, and AG346 were the twin starting points for the Mustang story, the latter being the first example to be delivered to Britain under the terms agreed by the British Purchasing Commission. Having made a few not so sound acquisitions of existing US aircraft, the commission and North American Aviation came up trumps by opting for a completely new fighter *(NAA via Merle Olmsted)*

Actual aerial co-operation with the British Army meant, at that stage of the war, endless training exercises. Few troops were about to undertake offensive operations, and in lieu of immediate battle commitments, the bulk of the regiments based in the UK could re-equip and develop new tactics, paying due regard to the lessons of the German *Blitzkreig*, which had all but revolutionised conventional land warfare. Exercises, some of them on a vast scale involving thousands of men and vehicles, became a regular activity. Air support, previously badly neglected, began to take on an increasing importance.

ACC squadrons soon demonstrated the value of tactical airpower to mobile ground forces and, in general, laid the foundation for what would later become a decisive factor in Allied victory. Utilising their own airborne 'eyes', Army Air Liaison Officers helped forge a vital air-ground partnership; Army involvement in this particular branch of the RAF extended to ground officers commanding units for certain periods.

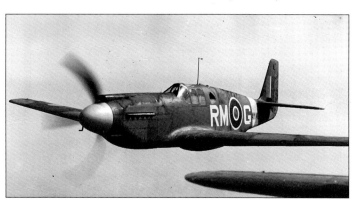

In January 1942 No 26 Sqn, based at Gatwick in Sussex, became the first RAF unit to be issued with the Mustang Mk I for operational trials. Almost immediately No 26 undertook two weeks' training at Weston Zoyland, and with this complete, 'A' Flight began Mustang conversion in earnest.

Mustang Mk I AM148 of No 26 Sqn was the subject of a series of recognition photos taken shortly after Army Co-operation Command (ACC) units began re-equipping with the type in 1942. Occasionally plagued by hostile attention from unwitting Allied pilots due to its similarity to the Bf 109, the Mustang was photographed from all angles and the results widely distributed throughout the RAF. This view clearly shows the overpainted rear canopy section which was so modified to reduce the amount of glare getting in to the lens of the F24 camera, located behind the pilot in the radio compartment. This particular Mk I was issued to No 309 Sqn after service with No 26, before finally ending its days at Rolls-Royce

To help the aircraft fulfil the armed recce role demanded by the ACC a single F24 camera for taking five-inch square oblique photographs was installed behind the pilot's seat above the radio sets in RAF Mustang Mk Is. The lens of this camera exposed to port via an aperture in the 'half-round' rear cockpit glazing, and some individual aircraft had this painted over to reduce glare. Various tests were made to determine the ideal altitude for photography, and Mustang pilots found they could generally achieve successful target coverage from an altitude of 9000 ft by holding the aircraft in a bank and aligning the camera with a mark made on the wing trailing edge.

A great number of potential targets lay in Occupied Europe and these needed to be extensively photographed for future attacks by both the RAF and the USAAF – the latter was due to begin long-range bomber operations from Britain that summer, hence the need for more recce observations. Three weeks before the first Eighth AAF B-17 raid, RAF Mustangs flew the first long-range reconnaissance on 27 July 1942 when 16 aircraft photographed the Dortmund-Ems Canal, a waterway important to the transportation system serving the factories of the Ruhr Valley.

Such forays eventually generated a vast visual panorama of enemy territory which quickly ran to thousands of high-quality prints for the target folders. These were distributed to RAF and USAAF commands, the ACC Mustang squadrons materially providing VIIIth Bomber Command with a great many of its early target photographs.

While 'pure' photographic briefings did not envisage the Mustang pilot having much need to use his guns, all sorties went out with the aircraft fully armed. Many flights across the Channel during this 'probing' period took the form of tactical *Rhubarb* sorties – small-scale harassing raids utilising cloud cover. These commenced for No 26 Sqn in May. Ground strafing by low-flying Mustangs began to yield a useful tally of equipment denied to the Germans, including a considerable quantity of supplies carried by river traffic.

Mustangs also flew numerous *Popular* sorties, this being the code name for general tactical reconnaissance against a variety of continental coastal targets of interest to the Army. As all these lay in otherwise friendly areas, each attack was carefully planned to minimise the risk of peripheral civilian casualties.

In general ACC Mustang pilots were briefed to avoid enemy aircraft rather than to endanger themselves, and their precious intelligence data, by seeking combat. Although the Mustang Mk I could give a good account of itself against the Fw 190 and Bf 109, it was pointless to risk pilots and aircraft unnecessarily. Naturally, the recon pilot did not always

have the choice if he happened to be bounced by the enemy.

In March 1942 No 241 Sqn received its first Mustang Mk Is, and in April Nos 16, 268 and 613 Sqns, were similarly re-equipped. The final unit issued the aircraft that month was No 2 Sqn, whose pilots at Sawbridgeworth, Essex, were eager to explore the Mustang's potential in combat, for it was easily the fastest and most modern machine the command had yet had a chance to fly. In common with other ACC squadrons, No 2 had previously been equipped with the Curtiss Tomahawk, which was often found wanting due to an inadequate performance and numerous technical troubles, many of them, ironically enough, stemming from the aircraft's Allison V-1710-33 engine, which was not overly dissimilar to that which powered the Mustang.

However, unlike its American predecessor, few pilots were disappointed in the Mustang. It was a delightful aircraft to fly, the low-altitude rated Allison engine giving a good power range and more than enough speed at the ceilings favoured by ACC units. Being officially sanctioned to enjoy the exhilaration of flying very low and fast in one of the world's best aircraft, ACC pilots accepted the inherent risks that left little room for error or technical malfunction. At last their little-publicised role had been given the right equipment to do the job, and many pilots could be forgiven for lauding the fact that low down they could outrun a Spitfire. Army co-operation flying may have lacked some of the 'glamour' of a fighter squadron, but it offered plenty of alternative forms of excitement!

Although single aircraft sorties were flown by some units, No 2 Sqn made it a rule always to send two Mustangs on patrol, one pilot concentrating on the designated mission while the other acted as a 'weaver' to

Once issued to ACC squadrons, the Mustang Mk I wrote a new chapter in the low-level coverage of continental targets via the camera lens. Many installations also felt the weight of the type's six M2 .50 cal machine guns as most RAF recce flights went out armed. These Mustang Mk Is carry the badge of the Guards Armoured Division on the nose, denoting the close liaison the squadrons maintained with individual regiments during the long-haul training period from 1942 to 1944 (*IWM*)

watch for enemy activity – particularly intercepting German fighters. To fully utilise the Mustangs' range capability, the squadron flew from a number of forward airfields apart from its main base – these included Coltishall, Fowlmere, Bottisham and Thruxton. To their chagrin, pilots found the accommodation on some stations to be in tent form, and on occasions the grass strips they were obliged to use were less than kind to their aircraft. All squadrons flying Mustang Mk Is suffered their share of accidents, but no more so that with any other type new to operational service. The fact that the Mustang had a wide track main undercarriage was appreciated in these situations as the narrower track of the Tomahawk had been one of the main causes of ground-looping.

Not all Mustang PR flights could be completed successfully, and German flak and fighters downed a substantial number of aircraft during lengthy wartime service. No 239 Sqn lost AG524/'HB-B' on an armed recce to the Bruges area on 14 August 1942. The carcass was duly examined by German troops, and some parts salvaged by a diligent enemy, who had a considerable stock of Mustang spares by war's end (*Bundesarchiv*)

In the early days the large majority of Mustang sorties were generated to photograph potential targets on the Dutch coast, an area that became a familiar haunt of RAF pilots. Unfortunately, the regular appearance of the low-flying Tac/R machines also enabled the Germans to site light and medium flak batteries accurately enough to shoot down a number of machines.

Along with *Populars* and *Rhubarbs*, Mustangs flew *Jim Crows* and *Shipping Jim Crows*, which were aimed at locating respective land and seaborne targets for subsequent attack. *Circuses* involved the Mustangs in bomber escort, and there were offensive fighter sweeps and shipping reconnaissance sorties dubbed *Lagoons*.

DIEPPE

By the time of the combined services 'dry-run' invasion, staged at Dieppe on 19 August 1942, there were 15 Mustang Mk I squadrons within the RAF, including No 309 *Ziemia Czerwienskiej* Sqn, the first Polish Air Force unit to fly this type. Having taken its first aircraft on charge in June, No 309, like the other Mustang units, was still in the process of re-equipping when the Tac/R wings were formed. Four squadrons – Nos 26, 239, 400 and 414, which comprised No 35 Wg – participated in Operation *Jubilee*, the Mustangs providing tactical reconnaissance in support of the landing forces. Based at Gatwick, the Wing was tasked with observing German troop movements on the routes into Dieppe.

The first sorties took off at 0435 on the 19th, and apart from a mid-morning lull, the Mustangs flew until 1315, some two hours after the survivors of the invasion force had begun to withdraw. Despite many valuable lessons being learned, the Dieppe 'reconnaissance in force' was a very costly exercise that adversely affected many of the air units, as well as the ground forces, involved. For example, nine Mustangs were lost – five from No 26 Sqn, two from No 239 and one from No 400.

Bringing down the 'low and fast' reconnaissance fighters was the responsibility of both the *Jagdwaffe* units tasked with patrolling the Dieppe area and the flak batteries sited in and around the port. A number of aerial skirmishes ensued, but in the main the Mustang's good rate of turn and speed prevented prohibitive losses being suffered as a result of enemy fighter attack – there were only ever 19 ACC Mustangs identified

Flg Off Hollis 'Holly' Hills puts his point across for the cameras following his combat success over an Fw 190 during the Dieppe landings on 19 August 1942. Hailing from Los Angeles, Hills was serving with No 414 Sqn, RCAF, at the time of his sole combat kill in Europe. He later scored four more victories whilst flying F6F-3 Hellcats with the US Navy's VF-32 aboard USS *Langley* in the Pacific in 1944 – see *Aircraft of the Aces 10 Hellcat Aces of World War 2* for more details (*Hollis Hills*)

as having been shot down by German fighters during the war, and even then six of this number contain a degree of uncertainty as to exactly how they were lost. Apart from those downed by flak, the fate of many more Mustang Mk Is that failed to return from combat was never definitely determined, and admittedly some of these are likely to have been destroyed by German fighters. The other side of the coin was confirmed victories over Luftwaffe fighters by the ACC units, and these too were modest in number, given the ruling to avoid combat wherever possible.

Fittingly, the first enemy aircraft officially credited to a Mustang Mk I fell to an American pilot serving in the RAF by the name of Flg Off Hollis 'Holly' Hills during a sortie to cover the Dieppe raid. A civilian pilot during the 1930s, he joined the RCAF in June 1940 and was posted to No 414 Sqn, initially on P-40 Tomahawks, in mid-1941. His following detailed account of the combat was first published in the Summer 1990 edition of the excellent US Naval Aviation journal *The Hook*.

'On the pitch black morning of 19 August 1942, Flt Lt Freddie Clark and I, as weaver, took off from Gatwick for a road recce from Abbeville (France) to Dieppe, checking for movement of German armour. How I was able to find Freddie in the dark I'll never know. There were no navigation lights and the join up was on the deck. I was stepped up on Freddie as we flew across the Channel just a few feet above the water. About half way across station keeping on Freddie's plane was made easy by the glow of AA fire and searchlights at Dieppe, where Bostons were attacking the heavy guns (opposing British amphibious raids). As soon as we crossed the coast, however, I lost sight of Freddie in the inky black and I had to finish the mission alone. I could make out nothing on the ground – no roads, no vehicle tracks, nothing.

'My second mission later that day was the same – weaver for Freddie, looking for German armour en route to Dieppe. The weather was sunny, not a cloud in the sky. As we approached the French coast, the sky was full of fighters in one massive dogfight from sea level to the contrail level. In hurried glances, I counted seven parachutes in the air at one time. A couple of miles short of landfall I spotted four Fw 190s off to our right at about 1500 ft. Their course and speed was going to put them directly overhead when we crossed the beach. I called Freddie twice with a "tally ho" but there was no response. He did not hear the warnings and apparently did not see the Fw 190s. When Freddie turned left under the enemy to intersect our target road, I tried to radio a warning to him again, but got no response. Once over our target, Freddie turned right for Abbeville, which put us in an ideal position for the Fws to attack. I swung very wide to Freddie's left during the turn, dusting the Abbeville chimney tops. That kept me beneath the Fws, and I believe they lost sight of me.

'My plan was to cut off the lead Fw 190 before he could open fire on Freddie, but my timing went to pot when a crashing Spitfire forced me to turn to avoid a collision. That gave the lead Fw pilot time to get into firing position and he hit Freddie's Mustang with the first burst. I got a long range shot at the Fw leader but had to break right when his number two man had a go at me. Number two missed and made a big mistake of sliding to my left side ahead of me. It was an easy shot and I hit him hard. His engine caught fire, and soon after it started smoking the canopy came off. I hit him again and he was a goner, falling off to the right into the trees.

'The second pair of Fw 190s had vanished so I raced toward Dieppe looking for Freddie's Mustang. I saw him heading for the harbour at 1000 ft, streaming glycol, with the lead Fw trailing behind. The Fw pilot started to slide dead astern Freddie so I gave him a short high-deflection burst to get his attention. He broke hard left into my attack and the ensuing fight seemed to go on forever. I could out turn him, very slowly gaining advantage, but just as I got into firing position he would break off and streak inland, using the superior power of his BMW engine. He would come back at me as soon as I turned to head for the coast and we'd start our turning competition all over again. During one turn I had to dodge a crashing plane – a Bf 109 – and the Fw pilot got his only shot at me. His deflection was too great and he missed, but I was impressed with the firepower of his 20 mm cannon. My opponent was a highly competent pilot and I was ready to call a draw as soon as I could.

'The timing of one of the Fw 190 breakaways was such that I got my Mustang up to speed and escaped to the coast, toward Dieppe. The Fw 190 didn't follow, there was no sign of Freddie, and I was fortunate not to get hit by AA fire as I crossed the harbour. Halfway across the Channel, I flew directly under a gaggle of Ju 88s and Bf 109s returning from an attack on Southampton. We ignored each other and the rest of my trip was without thrills. It was sombre that evening in the mess. Freddie was missing (our only loss), but the other Mustang units had taken severe losses. I went to bed in my quarters, and at about five the next morning, my door burst open. I was grabbed in a bear hug by what smelled like a huge clump of seaweed. It was Freddie. He'd ditched his Mustang in the Dieppe harbour and was rescued unconscious by a brave soldier of the amphibious forces. With Freddie as witness, the Fw 190 shootdown was confirmed for me and No 414 Sqn as the first Mustang kill.'

Hills was unable to add to his score, and with US forces now arriving in Britain in force, he was pressured into joining the Army Air Forces. He wanted to fly Spitfires with the Eagle Squadrons within the newly-created 4th FG, but was offered P-38s instead, so he joined the US Navy! Hills returned to America for training and eventually helped establish the FM Wildcat-equipped (later Hellcats) VF-32 in June 1943, with whom he scored four further kills. Relatively few pilots were able to claim confirmed victories with the early marks of Mustang in RAF service.

By October 1942 the previous pattern of Tac/R operations was revised slightly in that the Mustang force was henceforth engaged increasingly on

Cruising over Essex fields during a training flight from its Sawbridgeworth base in July 1942, this No 2 Sqn Mustang Mk I (AG633) still appears to be in remarkably fresh condition – this would soon change once the squadron became involved in Tac/R sorties in the lead up to Dieppe *(via Phil Jarrett)*

Rhubarbs. Given the prerequisite bad weather for such ops, it was the 21st before conditions were deemed right for the first mission of this new operational phase to be flown – four aircraft hit a German camp and Dutch shipping traffic. Other sorties also were flown during this period, with No 2 Sqn performing its first *Popular* on 2 November 1942 – by which time the RAF's Mustang strength had grown to 17 units. No 168, the last to re-equip that year, made its debut from Odiham on 7 December with a *Rhubarb* over Northern France. Further expansion of Tac/R Mustang strength saw No 430 Sqn receive aircraft in January 1943, with No 231 following suit in March, No 516 in April and No 14 in May.

While the RAF was writing the first part of the Mustang story, North American Aviation had received orders for a variant similar to the British Mk I for service with the US Army Air Force. Initial American deployment for the type was also envisaged in a tactical role, except that AAF close support units would also use Mustangs as attack/dive-bombers. In June 1942 500 examples were ordered as A-36As.

The RAF had no requirement for the A-36, with only one example being tested in the UK, but an improved Mk I with four 20 mm cannon was ordered as the Mustang Mk IA. Covering 150 aircraft, this order had not been completed by the time the Japanese attacked Pearl Harbor on 7 December 1941, and the subsequent US need for modern combat aircraft to suddenly fight a two-front war in the Pacific and Europe was to have an adverse effect on future deliveries of Mustangs to the RAF under the terms of the new Lend-Lease agreement.

Nevertheless, 150 Mustang Mk IAs arrived in Britain and these equipped six squadrons (Nos 2, 63, 168, 170, 171 and 268) to complement the Mk Is already in inventory. The type's four 20 mm Hispano cannon could deal with most types of target the Tac/R Mustangs were likely to encounter, and as this weapon was already in widespread use in British fighters, few maintenance problems were experienced.

To make good the shortfall of Mk IAs, the RAF subsequently received 50 P-51As diverted from USAAF contracts. Armed with four .50 in wing guns instead of cannon and fitted with racks for external stores, these machines were known as Mustang Mk IIs. While some pilots who flew this mark might have bemoaned the loss of the Hispano cannons' punch, the weight of fire from four heavy American machine guns usually proved more than adequate.

By the time the Mustang Mk II arrived in Britain in mid-1943, ACC

Sawbridgeworth was like many other satellite fields that sprung up across the south east corner of England as the war progressed – little more than a requisitioned farmer's field with the odd track and Nissen hut scattered here and there. 'U-XV', alias AG550, sits chocked in the summer sun at No 2 Sqn's dispersal in July 1942 *(via Phil Jarrett)*

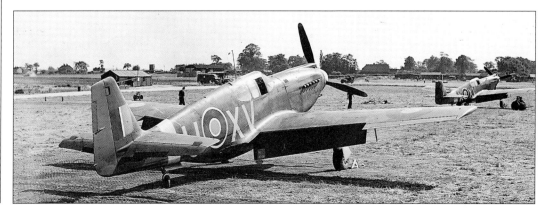

As the tide of the war turned in the Allies' favour, so the RAF went more on the offensive across Europe. As part of this escalation, the ACC's Mustangs were approved to carry bombs and rocket projectiles (RPs), with AG357/G being one of two Mk Is utilised in trials to clear underwing ordnance. This extensive ironmongery associated with the ubiquitous Unrotated Projectile (official Air Ministry jargon for 'rocket') failed to see operational service with the RAF's Allison-engined Mustang force, but was extensively fitted to the Mk IIIs, particularly in Italy (*via Phil Jarrett*)

had been disbanded (on 1 June) and the Tac/R Mustang squadrons were transferred either to Fighter Command or to the new 2nd Tactical Air Force (2nd TAF) to hone their air support training for the forthcoming invasion of Europe. Tactical reconnaissance of the continent became increasingly important and the Mk I/II force became an integral part of Nos 83 and 84 Gps which, with the squadrons of No 11 Gp, maintained the aerial offensive against continental targets until such time as an Allied land invasion could take place

During the autumn of 1943 the RAF Mustang squadrons were dispersed as follows: No 83 Gp, 39th (RCAF) Reconnaissance Wing had Nos 231 (RAF) and 400 (RCAF) Sqns at Redhill and Nos 414 (RCAF) and 430 (RCAF) which were at Gatwick. No 84 Gp strength included the 35th Reconnaissance Wing with Nos 2 and 4 Sqns at Thruxton and Nos 167, 170 and 268 Sqns at Odiham. All units flew Mustang Mk Is except Nos 168 and 268 Sqns, which had Mk IAs.

Earlier, in July 1943, a number of sorties flown by Tac/R Mustangs were aimed at intercepting aerial minsweepers. These *Haunch* sorties were intended to prevent Ju 52s, and the occasional naval vessel, from detonating Allied magnetic mines through the use of a degaussing ring but as far as the Luftwaffe's standard transport went, no successes were achieved, at least by the Mustangs.

With pilots permitted to operate up to 300 miles from their home bases on early *Rhubarbs*, the 1943 introduction of long-range wing drop tanks, each containing 62.5 Imp gal, enabled this radius of action to be doubled. Alternatively, the wing racks were stressed to take a 500-lb bomb on each side.

Mustang weaponry extended to eight 60-lb rocket projectiles (RPs) on underwing rails, tested on AM130/G and AG357/G, and although no Mk Is used RPs in action, this weapon was to see service in the Mediterranean with the Mk III. This necessary boost in RAF Mustang ground attack capability was not universally welcomed, however, as ordnance inevitably carried a weight penalty – despite its lack of altitude performance the 'clean' Mk I remained the lightest of the early Mustang series, and on this basis alone would have been preferred by some pilots on a straight comparison with later versions.

As things transpired, few pilots ever got the chance to compare the differing marks, for only one squadron previously equipped with the Allison Mustang – the Polish No 309 Sqn – was issued with the Mk III due to both the entirely different operating roles and flying characteristics of the two sub-types, as well as the sheer number of aircraft available. The latter factor tended to mitigate against the Tac/R squadrons for as attrition dwindled the available numbers of Mk Is, IAs and IIs, the RAF was faced with losing the kind of long-range coverage the Allison-engined aircraft had excelled at. North American had ceased production of early pre-Mer-

of early pre-Merlin series machines in mid-1943, in order to concentrate entirely on the P-51B which was so desperately needed for long-range escort by the Eighth Air Force.

This situation left the RAF with little alternative but to re-equip a number of Mustang Mk I squadrons with other types, despite the latter generally proving to be inferior tactical reconnaissance aircraft. Hawarden became something of an RAF Mustang centre when No 3 Tactical Exercise Unit was formed there on 11 November 1943, primarily to convert pilots who would be urgently required to fly invasion support sorties. Also equipped with Spitfires, the unit operated until March 1944, but was then relocated at Aston Down to continue Mustang conversion until war's end.

Those Mustang units that would support the invasion were slimmed down to the barest essentials to become almost autonomous, thus enabling them to operate under primitive conditions from forward airstrips. The Mustang units became part of an 'Airfield' which constituted a squadron nucleus built around its aircraft, pilots, a CO and adjutant, plus a small liaison section dependent for support on a mobile airfield team which was responsible for aircraft maintenance, refuelling, accommodation of personnel and so forth.

For the actual invasion, No 168 Sqn RAF and two RCAF units, Nos 414 and 430, flew Mustang Mk Is while No 400 RCAF, which had by then relinquished its Mustangs for Spitfire Mk XIs, completed the 39th Reconnaissance Wing of No 83 Gp, tasked with supporting the Second British Army. The First Canadian Army was served by No 84 Gp's 35th Recon Wing, comprising veteran ACC units Nos 2 and 268 Sqns with Mustang Mk IAs and IIs, while another ex-Mustang unit, No 4 Sqn, also now flew Spitfire Mk XIs.

——— FIGHTER COMMAND MK IIIS ———

Although RAF fighter squadrons were not equipped with the medium- to low-altitude Mustang Mk I, the successful installation of the Rolls-Royce Merlin in the P-51B airframe created an entirely different aircraft. The Mk III, which eventually equipped 22 RAF squadrons, offered not only an excellent all-round performance at altitude, coupled with improved armament and stores-carrying capability, but also an exceptional range for a single-seat fighter. RAF Mk IIIs were duly procured under Lend-Lease from US contracts, rather than being directly purchased as the Mk Is and IIs had been.

From the British viewpoint, the Mk III's only drawback was the modest armament of four Browning .50 in machine guns. These otherwise highly reliable weapons were awkwardly positioned at an angle in the P-51B's slim-profile wing bays, and gave the Americans considerable trouble when initially used in combat at height. British Mk IIIs generally operated at lower alti-

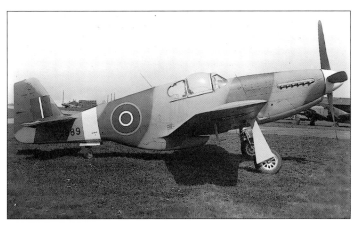

Factory-fresh and awaiting assignment to a frontline unit in the UK, Mustang Mk III FX889 sits at an anonymous ATC airfield surrounded by Oxfords in early 1944. Soon it would be issued to No 122 'Bombay' Sqn at Funtington, just north of Portsmouth, and adorned with both the unit's 'MT' codes and D-Day invasion stripes. It flew a considerable number of support missions for *Overlord* before heading across the Channel to B7/Martragny, east of Bayeux, on 26 June, accompanied by the rest of the unit *(via Phil Jarrett)*

The sleek lines of Mustang Mk III FZ149 of No 306 Sqn, seen here in post-invasion markings. The black and white stripes have been daubed over with a suitable dark shade to render them less conspicuous, a full repaint having to wait for a period of less intensive operations. This particular machine was issued to the Polish unit post-*Overlord* as an attrition replacement

tudes, and thus avoided icing-up, one of the biggest bugbears with AAF P-51B guns, but the installation nevertheless continued to give trouble.

A temporary shortage in P-51B/C deliveries to US VIIIth Fighter Command groups led to the transfer of 36 British-contract Mk IIIs during the period from December 1943 to January 1944, which slightly delayed the first RAF unit being declared operational until early 1944. These transferred machines were fitted with the British clear-view Malcolm cockpit hood, a feature much admired – and indeed coveted – by American pilots who otherwise had to make do with the original, heavily framed, 'greenhouse' canopy on their P-51B/Cs. Some Malcolm hoods found their way to AAF depots to be fitted to standard P-51Bs, but output of the canopies remained modest and relatively few US machines eventually boasted this modification – those aircraft that did were often preferred by their pilots to the P-51D.

No 65 Sqn based at Gravesend, in Kent, was the first Mustang Mk III unit, being declared operational on the new type in mid-February 1944. No 19 Sqn completed transition training at almost the same time, to be followed soon after by No 122 – these three squadrons then formed No 122 Wg.

By the spring of 1944 North American production had caught up with demand to the extent that the all-important escort of USAAF bombers from UK bases was being handled solely by Eighth Air Force P-51B/C groups, thus freeing the RAF to plan its own operations with Mustang Mk IIIs. Highly versatile, and capable of performing all types of fighter operations equally as well as, or better than, other types in service, the Mustang Mk III flew both high- and medium-level escort missions, as well as ground attack sorties.

The spring months of 1944 saw an increasing number of USAAF and RAF Mustangs operating from British airfields, the three squadrons of No 122 Wg being joined by a second wing, No 133, comprising Nos 129 RAF, 306 *City of Torun* and 315 *City of Deblin* PAF Sqns. RAF Mustangs spent the remaining months before the invasion escorting tactical operations across the Channel, and utilising their longer range capability to cover Coastal Command's more distant anti-shipping forays to the coastal regions of Holland, Norway and Germany. A seventh RAF fighter squadron, No 316 *City of Warsaw*, became the third Polish unit to fly the Mk III and to specialise in escorting Coastal's strike squadrons (then equipped primarily with Beaufighters), these operations beginning in April 1944. Considering the opposition the attackers often faced, a fighter escort was more than welcome.

OVERLORD SUPREMACY

By 6 June 1944 the mighty Allied fighter force built up in the UK was highly capable of covering the invading ground forces and preventing the Luftwaffe from disrupting Operation *Overlord* in the vital early hours. RAF Mustang Mk IIIs offered able support, primarily in a ground attack capacity, with the sortie rate demanded in the period immediately after

With facilities ready to refuel, rearm and bomb-up fighters for the next sortie, RAF Servicing Commandos also established local airfield defence. Here, at the rudimentary strip at B12/Ellon, a group of clean cut 'Tommies' have set up a card school behind a Bren gun position. In the background Mustang Mk III 'MT-A' of No 122 Sqn is bombed-up ready for its next sortie

Finless American 500-lb bombs sit secured to a trailer ready for hanging on Mustangs of No 306 Sqn. Providing that their individual weight was within limits, Mustangs could accommodate either British or US bombs. Note the typical rough application of the AEAF black and white stripes on the fuselage, although as per regulations the code letters have been masked off to remain readable (*PAF*)

the troops slogged their way ashore keeping the pilots very busy. On 8 June near Gace, No 65 Sqn was busy bombing German vehicles when four Fw 190s were spotted. Led by the OC, Kiwi Sqn Ldr Westenra (who finished the war with eight kills, including 2^1/3 on Mustang Mk IIIs), No 65's pilots enthusiastically gave chase and succeeded in shooting down two of the enemy machines, while the pilot of a third fighter baled out. Later that morning, No 19 Sqn attacked a motor convoy with guns and bombs.

Prospects for air combat remained limited, however, for the order of the day (from before dawn to dusk) for the Mustang Mk III squadrons was ground attack – bridges, vehicles, marshalling yards and river traffic were among the targets. Initially, pilots operated from England and used forward airstrips in Normandy for refuelling and rearming before returning home for the night. No 122 Wg eventually moved to France in late June.

By this stage in the invasion the Luftwaffe had finally begun to challenge Allied operations, and on 24 July one of the largest air battles to date took place when some 40 Fw 190s and Bf 109s encountered No 65 Sqn's Mustangs. Four of the latter were brought down for a score of nine German fighters.

During August, No 122 Wg's Mustangs were given the task of closing the River Seine to German barge traffic and on the 4th the wing dropped 166 1000-lb bombs plus 500-pounders on this target. 'Barge busting' continued unabated, and on the 10th No 19 Sqn shot down four Fw 190s during such an operation.

Another major clash between Mustang Mk IIIs and Fw 190s took place on 18 August when No 315 Sqn bounced 60 fighters taking off and landing at Beauvais airfield during a penetration sweep into occupied France. Led by 13-kill ace Sqn Ldr Eugeniusz Horbaczewski, the unit despatched 16 Fw 190s in 15 minutes, including three by the OC – this raised his Mustang tally to 5.5 kills, and his overall score to 16.5. Sadly, he was then shot down and killed himself.

While the RAF had anticipated committing its entire Mustang Mk III force to invasion support, the opening of the V1 offensive brought some changes. Instead of moving to France as planned, No 133 Wg, plus No 316 Sqn, remained in the UK and became part of Air Defence of Great

Britain, the new temporary name for Fighter Command. Squadrons equipped with the best interceptor fighters now began flying sorties under Operation *Diver*, the defence of the country against Hitler's *Vertungswaffen 1*. A cheap and effective weapon, the V1 threatened to devastate London, the main target for Luftwaffe units manning the launching sites in France, unless British defences could get its measure without delay.

Despite the fighter squadrons and massed AA guns forming a formidable defence ring which blunted the attack significantly, many

Part of the well-decorated Mk III (FB387/'PK-G') of No 315 Sqn, flown by Capt Eugeniusz Horbaczewski (second from left), who was photographed here with other squadron pilots at Brenzett in early August 1944. Days later the Polish ace was shot down and killed in a dogfight with 60 Fw 190s over France – he had destroyed three German fighters in the combat prior to his death (*Dr P Koniarek archive*)

bombs got through to dump a ton of high explosive on random, mainly civilian, targets. For fighter pilots, intercepting V1s was far more dangerous than attacking a conventional aircraft; bringing them down by cannon and machine gun fire usually required a full power dive and the expenditure of hundreds of rounds of ammunition (an average of 500 for a Mustang) before they exploded. Momentum was such that the pilot could not always avoid the mid-air explosion and damage to his aircraft from debris. Squadrons flying Mustangs enjoyed a slim advantage in this respect for the American fighter's performance was such that it was able to catch the tiny bombs in level flight, giving the pilot a slim chance to manoeuvre and avoid the full force of the detonation.

The leading V1 ace with No 316 Sqn was W/O Tadeusz Szymanski, who described the downing of one of his eight kills to Bob Ogley several years ago for inclusion in the H E Bates volume *Flying Bombs over England*. His unit had moved to Friston from West Malling on 11 July in order to be right in the path of any incoming V1s, and the following day he was flying just such an anti-*Diver* patrol over the Channel, near Dungeness, when he was vectored onto an incoming flying bomb heading for Hastings. In a matter of minutes Szymanski had placed his Mustang within striking distance of his dull grey quarry, and closed in for the kill.

'I started shooting and saw strikes before my ammunition was finished, but the bomb kept on a dead-level course. Over the town of Hastings I moved into close formation to get a close look at it. The thing was jerking along and the elevator was flapping with each vibration of the crude jet motor. I noticed there were no ailerons, and on the front of the bomb was a silly little propeller. It looked ridiculous. We didn't know at the time but this was the arming device for the warhead, set to explode when the bomb hit the ground after so many miles.

'I decided to try and tip the "doodlebug" up with my wing tip. The flight was controlled by gyroscopes and if you turn a gyroscope more than 90° it goes haywire. As soon as I put my port wing under the "doodlebug's" wing, it started lifting and I banked to starboard. I repeated this manoeuvre 11 times but each time it went over so far and then came back.

An anonymous pilot sits in his well-marked Mustang Mk III, this time from No 306 Sqn. The Polish Air Force badge is carried forward of the pilot's score, which denotes four V1 silhouettes – he narrowly missed becoming a *Diver* ace, but five kills previously scored over conventional enemy aircraft brought that personal achievement (*Dr P Koniarek archive*)

Care is exercised by armourers of No 315 Sqn as they ensure the correct alignment of the ammunition belts in the feed tracks for the Mustang Mk III's four .50 cal guns, thus helping to avoid any in-flight firing jams. In general, lower altitude operations in warmer air tended not to create too many problems with these guns for the RAF, unlike the troubles that the USAAF experienced on bomber escort missions (*Dr P Koniarek archive*)

FB145 of No 315 Sqn is being bombed-up for a mid-1944 sortie – bomb graffiti wishing the enemy ill was very popular, but such comments were understandably most heartfelt by Poles. This Mk III flew with the unit from April through to July 1944, before suffering Category A damage in a flying accident on the 22nd of that month. It was in fact the oldest Mustang in the squadron at the time of the mishap (*Dr P Koniarek archive*)

By now the barrage balloons protecting London were in sight and I was becoming rather anxious.

'I tried a different manoeuvre, hitting it very hard with my wing tip as I went up into a loop. When I recovered my position I found, to my dismay, that the doodlebug was flying perfectly safe and level – but upside down! Suddenly it dived out of control and crashed in open countryside.'

In the three months No 316 Sqn were tasked with anti-*Diver* operations the unit accounted for 74 flying bombs, producing six V1 aces in the process. Aside from his eight V1s, W/O Tadeusz Szymanski also claimed 1¹/₂ kills against manned aircraft.

Mustang squadrons in general did well against the doodlebug menace, their combined score of at least 258, including five for the USAAF's 363rd Fighter Group (FG), making the Mk III/P-51B the third most effective type after the Spitfire Mk XIV and Tempest Mk V. Of the total pilots credited with five or more flying bombs destroyed, thereby making them *Diver* aces, 21 flew Mustangs, and not surprisingly, the scoreboard was dominated by the names of 16 Polish nationals. No 129 Sqn kept a tally of its V1 kills in an appropriate manner by recording them on a section of flying bomb wing. Below the squadron crest were stencilled rows of miniature bombs, similar to those that appeared on aircraft, each denoting a victory.

Back in France, No 122 Wg was making a significant contribution to the liberation of Europe, and among the statistics of enemy losses credited to the three squadrons was a score of 72 enemy aircraft destroyed from D-Day to 11 August. In addition, the wing claimed two probables and 41 damaged. More than 100 German aircraft had actually been shot down by No 122 Wg since its formation, and it was therefore decided to hold a sweepstake to reward the pilot who claimed the 122nd. In the event, the figure was exceeded during a combat on 20 August when Nos 19 and 65 Sqns were engaged by two-dozen Fw 190s some 20 miles east of Paris. In the ensuing melée the RAF pilots claimed nine Fw 190s shot down, three of them falling to Flt Lt L M A Burra-Robinson of No 65 Sqn – this trio of kills made him a Mustang Mk III ace, as he had previously downed a pair of He 111s at Dole and Tavaux airfields on 23 April 1944 whilst on a sweep with No 122 Sqn. This put the Wing's score over the 122 mark, with the result that the nine victories went into a hat and Flt Sgt Abbott of No 19 Sqn emerged the winner.

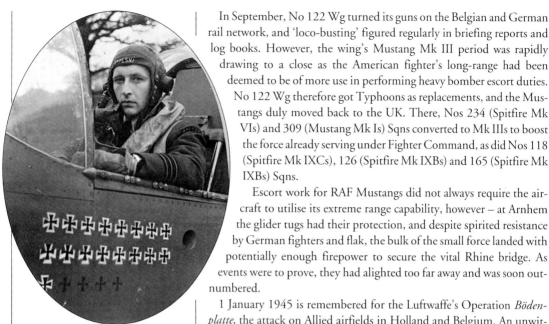

When it came to destroying German aircraft, few pilots could match the record of Stanislaw Skalski, who shot down 22 to become the highest scoring Polish pilot of the war. Only two of these were achieved while flying a Mustang III, however, (a pair of Bf 109Gs that collided without the Pole firing a shot on 24 June 1944!) the bulk of Skalski's victories being on Spitfires. By the time this shot was taken in mid-1944 Skalski had risen to the rank of Lieutenant Colonel, and was in charge of No 133 Wg at Northolt. Here, he is seen sitting in 'his' Mk III preparing for an inspection by HM King George VI at the Middlesex base
(*Dr P Koniarek archive*)

In September, No 122 Wg turned its guns on the Belgian and German rail network, and 'loco-busting' figured regularly in briefing reports and log books. However, the wing's Mustang Mk III period was rapidly drawing to a close as the American fighter's long-range had been deemed to be of more use in performing heavy bomber escort duties. No 122 Wg therefore got Typhoons as replacements, and the Mustangs duly moved back to the UK. There, Nos 234 (Spitfire Mk VIs) and 309 (Mustang Mk Is) Sqns converted to Mk IIIs to boost the force already serving under Fighter Command, as did Nos 118 (Spitfire Mk IXCs), 126 (Spitfire Mk IXBs) and 165 (Spitfire Mk IXBs) Sqns.

Escort work for RAF Mustangs did not always require the aircraft to utilise its extreme range capability, however – at Arnhem the glider tugs had their protection, and despite spirited resistance by German fighters and flak, the bulk of the small force landed with potentially enough firepower to secure the vital Rhine bridge. As events were to prove, they had alighted too far away and was soon outnumbered.

1 January 1945 is remembered for the Luftwaffe's Operation *Bödenplatte*, the attack on Allied airfields in Holland and Belgium. An unwitting observer of the carnage wreaked at Eindhoven was W/O Jack Lown of No 65 Sqn. Flying a lone radio relay sortie for the US heavy bombers which were very active that day, Lown was at 17,000 ft over the Dutch airfield when he saw the 'unusual amount of activity' as the German fighters worked-over the base.

Mustang losses to the strafing *Jagdflieger* totalled just three destroyed and one damaged at Eindhoven, these all being aircraft of No 39 Recce Wg. On that date RAF Tac/R Mustangs were additionally based at Gilze-Reijen with No 268 Sqn (Mk IA and II) and with No 2 Sqn (Mk IIs) under No 35 Recce Wg. Added to the losses inflicted by the Germans the resultant confusion led to some mistakes in recognition and a Mustang destroyed a Typhoon over Gilze-Reijen! All other P-51 casualties on 1 January were from the Eighth Air Force.

GESTAPO HUNTERS

On 21 March 1945 31 Mk IIIs and IVs drawn from Nos 64, 126 and 234 Sqns provided escort to a force of Mosquitos briefed for a vital operation – the destruction of records of Allied agents compiled by the Gestapo and stored at the Shell Haus, their HQ in the centre of Copenhagen. In addition a number of prisoners under sentence of death were incarcerated in the building, which was surrounded by civilian dwellings. The operation, which required pin-point bombing, was an outstanding success in that the main target was bombed, most of the records were destroyed, Gestapo personnel were killed and most of the prisoners managed to escape.

The Mustangs were tasked primarily with protecting the Mosquitos from German fighters, as well as to act as flak suppressors. Two Mk IIIs were lost, both from No 64 Sqn – an aircraft flown by Flt Lt David Drew was shot down by flak over Copenhagen, and the pilot killed, while a second aircraft crash-landed at Tarm, its pilot, Flg Off R Hamilton, being taken prisoner.

By early 1945, new Mustang Mk IVs were arriving in the UK for the

RAF, these joining the Mk IIIs on an 'as required' basis, rather than as replacements, to maintain squadron strength. The majority of the late-model Mustangs to don British markings were Dallas-built P-51Ks fitted with the Aeroproducts airscrew in place of the Hamilton Standard of the P-51D. A total of 597 Mk IVs was taken on RAF charge, and ultimately 15 squadrons were equipped, some not converting until hostilities ceased.

No 611 West Lancashire Sqn went operational on Mk IVs on 25 March 1945, and the Canadian Nos 441 and 442 followed suit in April, just in time to fly a number of long range-bomber escorts. On 9 April No 442 was part of a large force of ten Mustang and seven Spitfire squadrons which covered 53 Lancasters bound for the submarine yards and oil refineries at Hamburg. The Luftwaffe opposition was unusually strong that day, and ten miles from the target eight Me 262s dived on the bombers. Polish pilots reacted well to the threat and No 309 Sqn destroyed three jets and damaged others, while four more were claimed as damaged by Mustang pilots of Nos 64 and 306 Sqns.

The following day RAF Mustangs again fought with Me 262s whilst escorting Lancasters and Halifaxes bombing Leipzig's marshalling yards. Although the RAF fighters could not prevent the loss of two bombers to flak, Flg Off John 'Slops' Haslope, an Australian flying with No 165 Sqn, had cause to celebrate – when an Me 163 put in an appearance, Haslope firewalled his throttle to catch it. Diving after the rocket fighter and firing at it, his Mustang Mk III made a valiant attempt to follow the German pilot's violent pull-up, but the 'G' forces caused the Aussie to black out. Coming to at 8000 ft, Haslope realised that his aircraft was handling distinctly oddly.

Having made it back to Bentwaters, the pilot's Mustang was found to have several more degrees of dihedral than specified, plus severe wrinkling of the wing skin! It was not long before the results of the combat were known: a number of eye-witnesses among the bomber crews had seen the *Komet* dive into the ground, apparently out of control and disabled by Haslope's fire. Awarded the DFC for this action, Haslope thus became the only Commonwealth fighter pilot to be credited with an Me 163 victory. It was also the seventh, and last, *Komet* to fall to Mustang pilots between August 1944 and April 1945, all the others being USAAF kills.

No 303 *Warsaw-Kosciusko* Sqn just managed to fly the Mustang Mk IV

With barely 20 hours on the clock, an unmarked Mustang Mk IV radiates in its natural metal finish at an anonymous airfield in Britain in early 1945. Parked in the distance is another Mk IV, plus a USAAF P-38 (*via Phil Jarrett*)

operationally before war's end when, on 25 April, along with the four other Polish-manned Mk III units, they escorted Lancasters to Hitler's mountain retreat at Berchtesgarden, in Bavaria. Fittingly, this operation, which was even more of a Polish show in that 14 of the Lancasters were crewed by members of No 300 *Mazowiecki* Sqn, was the last for the PAF Mustang contingent, which had established an exemplary record whilst fighting in exile in Britain.

PERSONAL RECOLLECTIONS

Stan Farmiloe, a pilot with No 234 Sqn in the last 12 months of the war, recalls details of his unit's Mustang experience in the following interview conducted specially for this volume.

'No 234 Sqn received its Mustang Mk IIIs whilst at North Weald at the end of September 1944. Previously, the squadron had flown the Spitfire Mk VI and VB – the latter version being fondly referred to as "clipped, clapped and cropped" – otherwise very manoeuvrable, quite slow (in comparison with the Mustang) and very cold when flying at altitude due to there being no controlled heating. My last flight in a Spitfire Mk VB was on 25 September, and my first in a Mustang Mk III took place five days later.

'From my log book, I note that the longest trips made in Mk IIIs were as escorts for Lancasters bombing transformers in Munich on 9 April 1945 (4 hours and 50 minutes), and the Shell Haus raid to Copenhagen on 21 April, at 5 hours and 10 minutes. These were very long flights for single-seat aircraft, and of course greatly exceeded the range available with the Spitfire Mk V.

'We at no time had any trouble with the .50 in machine guns in either the Mk III or IV, but then again, as far as No 234 Sqn was concerned, we were never called upon to fly at high altitude. Certainly, for ground strafing the guns were most effective.

'Our main concern when flying Mustangs was the near-impossibility of making a safe ditching – and we almost daily flew at zero feet across the North Sea to Denmark and Holland. A Spitfire could be safely ditched, but we never heard of a Mustang pilot surviving such a forced landing.'

As a squadron that had flown Spitfires solidly from March 1940 until the arrival of the North American fighter in September 1944, the former type was understandably much loved by the pilots of No 234, but they soon realised that the Mustang was a much more effective weapon of war. By the time the unit re-equipped, dogfights with German fighters had become a rarity, but Stan Farmiloe believes that faced with aerial combat, pilots would have been equally at home in either type. Had individual pilots been obliged to choose between the two, some would have opted for a Spitfire for its manoeuvrability, others a Mustang, primarily for its high speed – but overall the squadron welcomed the change to the excellent American fighter.

One manifestation of Allied superiority over the Luftwaffe was the American decision to abandon camouflage paint in favour of 'natural metal finish' during 1943. A practical move that reduced drag, unpainted frontline aircraft were not so readily accepted by the RAF, which had a number of its Mk IV (P-51D) and Mk IVA (P-51K) Mustangs camouflaged after delivery. In this poor quality, but nevertheless interesting, view camouflaged No 19 Sqn Mk IVs formate on a B-25 Mitchell, the former being led by unpainted KM182, flown by Gp Capt D Ross-Shore, OC No 239 Wg in 1945

ARMY MUSTANGS OVER EUROPE

Abelated realisation by the USAAF that the Mustang could undertake a useful reconnaissance role for the Army Air Forces along similar lines to those of the RAF led to the first 'American' P-51As arriving in the UK in October 1943. As the British had earlier found in 1942, the tactical reconnaissance role in Europe demanded a fighter with a performance at least

as good as the early Mustang, and RAF methods were more or less copied by the Americans, using aircraft that were virtually identical, but fitted with US-manufactured K24 cameras. So it was that 24 P-51As (configured as F-6As) were despatched to the 67th Tactical Reconnaissance Group (TRG) based at Membury. Then part of the Eighth Air Force, the 67th was subsequently transferred to the Ninth, where the F-6As flew the first *Popular* sorties on 20 December.

AAF chiefs were even more thorough than their RAF contemporaries in dissuading their pilots from 'mixing it' with enemy fighters, an order that did not hang well on the shoulders of young men who had a very good aircraft, an aggressive spirit and magazines full of ammunition! As the tac recon task widened after D-Day, individual pilots made a name for themselves by scoring kills over the Luftwaffe, as well as carrying out their primary task, and a number achieved ace status. For example, on D-Day the 67th TRG's 15th TRS claimed, in addition to its regular reconnaissance duties, the destruction of three enemy aircraft.

In total five tactical reconnaissance pilots were officially credited with scores high enough to make them aces, Clyde B East coming top with 13 kills. Like East, three others – John Hoefker (8.5), Leland Larson (6) and Joe Waits (5.5) – flew with the 10th TRG, while Valentine Radar, with 6.5, was a member of the 67th TRG.

Although some AAF reconnaissance squadrons retained the F-4 and F-5 Lightning, with the F-3 Havoc and other types being available for special duties, the F-6 Mustang became the dominant type. Included in AAF reconnaissance squadrons' inventory were standard P-51s as well as photo-ships, particularly towards the end of the war when there were ample aircraft on hand and, conversely, the number

An F-6B of the 107th TRS/67th TRG, the AAF unit that first operated a version of the Mustang in the ETO. Going operational with the F-6A in October 1943, the 67th therefore beat the 354th to this distinction by about two months. And that its aircraft were flown fully armed with both cameras and guns is clearly demonstrated by the three kills marked on 42-103622 (*Olmsted*)

As the Allied fighter units moved forward to occupy former German airfields, increasing evidence of the demise of the Luftwaffe was found in the form of aircraft abandoned due to air attack, repair work for often minor damage not being completed before a pull-back was initiated – this Ju 88 looks definitely Cat E, however. Parked behind the burnt out wreck is an F-6B of the 15th TRS, with other Mustangs from the unit dispersed around the field in the background (*USAF*)

of tactical targets not already covered had significantly declined. It was during this final phase of the Allied advance into Germany that individual recon pilots met the Luftwaffe in the air, some of them getting their first taste of aerial combat. One such individual was 'Joe' Woods. Not officially listed as an ace, Woods nevertheless claimed five victories.

COVERING THE BOMBERS

With its initially-assigned P-51B Group (354th FG) on loan to the Eighth Air Force for the immediate future from December 1943, the Ninth Air Force, which had been re-established in England on 16 October, began medium bomber operations almost immediately. Born in the Mediterranean as the strategic bombing spearhead of an American campaign in Southern Europe, the Ninth was now to be fully equipped with medium and light bombers, fighters and fighter-bombers to support the North-Western European air offensive and, in due course, an invasion of France.

With the 354th FG 'Pioneers' otherwise engaged for the time being, the Ninth also lost its second P-51 group when the 357th was 'traded' to the Eighth as a second long-range escort group. In return, the Ninth AAF got the 358th, which had arrived in England to fly P-47s. Having been directly assigned the 362nd and 365th, both of which also flew Thunderbolts, the Ninth Air Force finally got a Mustang group it could retain in the shape of the 363rd. Little time was wasted in getting the 363rd into combat, as the Group flew its first ETO mission on 24 February, a 42-ship sweep over France and the Low Countries. By March the first enemy aircraft had been shot down.

The 363rd operated out of Rivenhall, Essex, and its first missions were led by Jim Howard, on loan from the 354th. Howard was not impressed with what he found; the 363rd had trained hard in the US on the P-39 Airacobra and had had, like the 354th, scant little Mustang conversion time. Unlike the 'Pioneers', however, the 363rd suffered a number of accidents directly attributable to a lack of pilot familiarisation with the P-51B. Its early sorties were also plagued by a high number of abortions on each mission, which tended to reduce effectiveness and colour the Group's performance, leading pilots to feel they were operating in the shadow of the 354th's success.

On the credit side, the 363rd often provided close escort to bomber formations, and did not in the main send its fighters ranging far ahead to blunt a *Jagdwaffe* attack before it developed. However successful such tactics by other groups were, a few German fighters invariably got through to hit the bombers from close range and the 363rd was there to deter them. Such work did not of course provide many chances for the 363rd's pilots to rack up impressive victory tallies, and this too was a contributory factor in what some saw as a poor performance. A similar situation occurred in the Eighth

Second top-scoring recon pilot of the ETO was Capt John Hoefker, who downed 8.5 kills during his tour with the 15th TRS in 1944/45. The majority of these victories were against Bf 109Gs and Fw 190s, and although he was pipped for top spot by Clyde East, Hoefker gained the distinction of being the first TRS pilot to make ace – a feat he achieved following a 3.5 kill mission on 17 December 1944 (*Hoefker via Murphey*)

John Hoefker's first three kills were scored in this 'plain Jane' F-6C, which also carries an extensive recon sortie log beneath its exhaust stubs. The camera fitted behind the seat shooting through the rear transparency is clearly visible in this shot. Aside from his air combat and photo recce exploits, Hoefker was also decorated with a second DFC for a series of perilous close support missions he flew during the Battle of the Bulge in defence of the besieged town of Bastogne – he was shot down twice in a week during this action (*Hoefker via Murphey*)

Air Force with the 356th FG, so the 363rd was not unique – someone had to keep close to the bombers and reassure their crews, preferably by staying in visual range. By far the worst problem experienced by pilots of the 363rd, however, was weather. Few groups appear to have run into

such appalling conditions as did this unfortunate outfit, and there is still speculation as to whether some losses – where missing pilots and their aircraft were never found – were attributable to the Germans or to collision in dense cloud. A substantial number were lost to this singular cause.

While it was logical for P-47s to predominate in the Ninth, few could disagree that the P-51 made an equally good ground attack aircraft, with the reservation that the Thunderbolt's big air-cooled radial engine was marginally less susceptible to damage by ground fire than the Mustang's

P-51B 43-12216 of the 356th FS, 354th FG 'hurdles' the overcast during one of the first P-51B escort sorties ever flown. It was not long before the 'Pioneer' Mustang Group adopted the white recognition markings that helped reduce accidents in the crowded skies of England during mission form up (*Olmsted*)

liquid-cooled Merlin. Production was the real key, and the availability of both fighters in ample numbers would reach the point where there were enough P-51s to meet the needs of both the Ninth and the Eighth, the diverse operational requirements of the two air forces notwithstanding. Along with the Mustang and Thunderbolt, the Ninth ably deployed the P-38 Lightning with the 370th FG, which went operational on 1 May 1944.

Eventually, most Ninth Air Force Groups largely standardised on the P-47, with the exception being the 474th which retained its P-38s, the type that originally equipped the 367th before it too changed to the Thunderbolt. Of the P-51 units, the 354th was obliged, in November 1944, to relinquish its Mustangs for P-47s for about three months.

The Allied spring 1944 offensive against tactical targets on the continent saw the Ninth's bomber groups heavily committed; fighters were kept busy on escort duty and sweeps, many of which resulted in a steady, if not spectacular, increase in air combat victories. The lion's share of these naturally enough fell to the recently returned 354th, whose pilots achieved ace status at an admirable rate, and conceded little to their more battle weary colleagues in the Eighth, many of whom had been in action considerably longer.

The second P-51B fighter group assigned to the Ninth was the 363rd, which the UK-based tactical air force managed to retain under its control, although the outfit also flew long-range escort missions for Eighth Air Force 'heavies' on many occasions. Numerous ground attack sorties were flown by the 363rd, this bombed up B-model being part of the 382nd FS. It subsequently became the personal aircraft of the CO, Maj Robert C McWherter, and re-coded 'C3-M' was christened *Hoo Flung Dung* (*Olmsted*)

This less than garish P-51B (42-106465) of the 380th FS was named *Maggie's DRAWERS* by its pilot, and it is seen here flying a training sortie over England during 1944

Throughout most of its existence in the ETO, the Ninth Air Force was known for flamboyant aircraft markings. The 356th FS's white stars on a blue band nose marking was particularly distinctive, and is shown to good advantage here on P-51B 43-7155/'AJ-H' landing at St Dizier, France, in September 1944. Nicknamed *Dorene*, the aircraft also has four kill markings painted below its cockpit (*J V Crow*)

As is well known, it was the P-51 that made 'all the way' bomber escort a reality and sowed the seeds of final, irrevocable, defeat for the Luftwaffe fighter force. Matching the Fw 190 and Bf 109 on nearly every count, a well-handled P-51B was a formidable weapon, although the early missions brought AAF groups more than their share of technical malfunctions, many of them weather-related. But the type's range superiority over any other fighter, Axis or Allied, was crystal clear, and in time the main technical problems were solved.

One that was harder to overcome was the similarity of the 'razorback' Mustang to the Bf 109. Bomber gunners particularly had scant little time to mull over the finer points of recognition, and some fighters came home with damage inflicted by weapons that had definitely not been made in Germany! Friend/foe recognition in the split seconds available to aircrew in combat remained a problem throughout the war, and Mustangs of the Ninth copied the Eighth AAF lead in adopting the type recognition stripes that undoubtedly saved a number of lives.

White-starred Mustangs were never totally immune from attack by other US fighters, however, and most combat records contain the occasional skirmish with friendlies flown by pilots more eager to nail a '109' than to study aircraft recognition. Fortunately, such encounters did not result in a high number of fatalities, but at the time they must have enraged harassed group commanders, and led to heated debate.

To place it nearer the action across the Channel, the 363rd FG moved to Staplehurst, Kent, on 14 April, four days before taking the bombers to Berlin. The group was redesignated the 363rd Fighter Bomber Group on 20 May, and on the 26th its pilots showed their mettle against the *Jagdflieger* by coming home with a tally of 12-4-6.

REORGANISATION

As the clock moved towards the date of the invasion, the Ninth Air Force reorganised its command structure and created, on 18 April, IX and XIX Tactical Air Commands (TACs), each to provide air support for a separate US Army once the Allies were established on the continent. As well as providing the bulk of the transports and gliders for the *Overlord* airborne forces, the Ninth AAF fully deployed its fighter-bombers, medium and attack bombers during the vital first days

With the beachhead secured and troops moving inland, Army engineers sought sites for very basic emergency fighter strips, and by 8 June the first one was ready for use. More permanent facilities were

25

available at Advanced Landing Grounds (ALGs), each with an initial letter prefix and code number which aircrew were advised to memorise, thus avoiding having to contend with verbally difficult local names, and the added risk of mispronunciation. A-3 at Cardonville was the first operational ALG, opened on 19 June – dozens more would be employed by Allied aircraft as the advance made progress across France and Belgium. Later, captured German airfields were similarly coded and the total list eventually ran into hundreds.

As part of the *Overlord* plan, fighter squadrons in IX TAC had responsibility for protecting the US 1st Army in France while XIX TAC, which included both P-51 groups, operated from England until such time as units could move across the Channel to continental airfields. The 354th occupied A-2 on 23 June, while advanced echelons of the 363rd had moved to A-7 (Azeville) the previous day.

In the meantime, the start of the V1 offensive against England had begun. This slightly delayed the 363rd's move across the Channel, and a P-51B flown by Capt James Dalglish duly destroyed the first robot bomb credited to the Group on 19 June. The 363rd continued to be deployed against the V1 menace for a few weeks, and successes were achieved on the 25th, 27th and 29th of that month. Consequently, it was 4 July before the 363rd's Mustangs appeared over ALG-15 Maupertus, their new base in France.

While the 363rd was to undertake numerous ground support missions in the coming weeks, it too tangled with the Luftwaffe on occasion. One of its pilots, whose name might not have been very well known at the time, opened his score on 25 June with a half share in the destruction of

Down in France at Maupertus or Azeville some time after the invasion, P-51D-5 *FOOL'S PARADISE IV* (44-13309) of the 380th FS/363rd FG has its upper surface AEAF stripes overpainted with olive drab paint in the field. Maj Evan McCall flew this P-51 until he rotated home after 36 ETO missions (*USAF*)

Maj Robert C McWherter served as the 382nd FS's CO for much of 1944, and flew P-51D 44-13380 *HOO FLUNG DUNG/CITY of PARIS* during the second half of the year. A seasoned campaigner who had scored kills over the Japanese in 1942/43, McWherter also enjoyed moderate success against the Luftwaffe – some of these kills must have been strafing claims as he fails to appear in the official ace listings for the USAAF (*Miller via Ivie*)

The centre section of P-51D 'A9-A' (44-13718) of the 380th FS provides the backdrop for a group of squadron pilots photographed in France during 1944 (*via Mackay*)

The last of the quartet of aces produced by the 15th TRS was the little-known Lt Joe Waits. He finished the war with 5.5 kills, learning his dogfighting craft from his flight leader, John Hoefker, during the Battle of the Bulge (*Williams via Ivie*)

The greatest recon ace of them all, Capt Clyde East scored an impressive 13 kills during his long tour with the 15th TRS. Prior to joining the Ninth AAF, he had served for five months in 1943 with No 414 Sqn RCAF, again flying Tac/R missions over Europe in Mustang Mk Is. Most of East's kills fell to the guns of this Mustang in the frantic last weeks of combat over Germany in April 1945 (*East via Ivie*)

an Fw 190. This individual was James Jabara, who was credited with another Fw 190 on 13 August, and who later served with the 355th FG. Jabara's greatest claim to fame, of course, came almost a decade later in the Korean War, a conflict from which he emerged as the second-highest ranking USAF Sabre ace with 15 kills (for his full story see *Aircraft of the Aces 4 - Korean War Aces* by Dorr, Lake and Thompson).

A combat on 18 July resulted in the 363rd's P-51s getting aerial claims of 10-0-5, a fine record and one which was repeated on too few occasions for the pilots' liking. And as if the 363rd had not been unfortunate enough, higher authority tended to deny victory claims by certain pilots, with the result that while several reached four, and a pair (Capt Richard W Asbury and Lt Bruce W Carr) who had already shot down enemy aircraft while flying combat with other groups made ace by scor-

ing one of two while they were with the 363rd, no pilot assigned wholly to the Group was confirmed as an ace during the war.

As Ninth AAF fighters interdicted and isolated the various battlefield areas it was gun emplacements, tanks, troops, locomotives, river traffic and bridges, rather than German aircraft, that were their targets, day in day out, for weeks. The Luftwaffe was generally unable to disrupt these operations, although the fighter *Gruppen* moved into forward French airfields offered what resistance they could against daunting odds.

Having done its share of bomber escort and ground attack work, the 363rd FG's days as a fighter unit were nevertheless numbered for on 4 September it became a recon group in IX TAC. In reality, little changed, as the 363rd TRG still flew P-51s – albeit F-6 photo-ships – in the same theatre of war and against much the same type of target. However, sorties now required the pilots to additionally take pictures and note anything of interest. Individuals who did not relish becoming Tac/R pilots were offered the choice of leaving the 363rd at this point to join the 354th, or

John Hoefker's F-6D 44-14597 sits amongst the puddles at a damp St Dizier airfield in France in late 1944. A camera port can just be seen cutting into the fuselage 'star and bar'. The 15th TRS refrained from adopting bright unit markings until well into 1945, as '5M-A' clearly shows (*Hoefker via Ivie*)

Clyde East is joined by a member of his groundcrew for a 'jolly' from Furth, Germany, in May 1945, just days after the cessation of hostilities. His full score is painted below the cockpit of *Lil' Margaret*, which also wears the checkerboard nose and tail stripes adopted by the 15th TRS earlier in the year – compare the unit markings of this machine with Hoefker's, pictured above (*East via Ivie*)

other fighter groups in the Ninth.

Upon becoming a tactical reconnaissance group, the 363rd's three fighter squadrons were renumbered – the 380th FS became the 160th TRS, the 381st FS the 161st TRS and the 382nd FS the 162nd TRS. Equipped with the F-6 (some of which were existing group P-51Ds field-modified to accommodate cameras), each squadron retained its old identifying code letters, and as was common practice amongst US tac recon groups, a fourth squadron was added – the 33rd PRS, equipped with F-5 Lightnings.

BATTLE OF THE BULGE

By October 1944 the Allied armies were spread all along the German border from east to west, although some areas were held by the minimum force deemed necessary. The month saw much destruction of the enemy's rail network, a percentage of it succumbing to the machine gun fire and bombs hauled by 354th Mustangs. And to the relief of many pilots, the group still met the Luftwaffe.

As autumn turned into winter the weather gradually deteriorated, thus slowing the Allied advance until by early December progress towards a vital Rhine crossing was almost at a standstill. Two weeks into the month came von Rundstedt's sudden armoured thrust through the Ardennes. The weight of the German offensive, spearheaded by carefully hoarded Tiger tanks which completely out-gunned anything in the Allied arsenal, took weakly-held US Army positions by surprise. Under cover of heavy snowfalls and mist that kept tactical aircraft on the ground, the panzers blasted a 60-mile 'bulge' into the frontline, their ultimate – and highly optimistic – objective being the port of Antwerp.

However, once the weather cleared, the Germans were unable to exploit their gains as Allied air superiority began to slowly restore the situation. By the time the besieged town of Bastogne was finally relieved following stubborn resistance in the face of overwhelming German forces, Hitler's desperate gamble had been neutralised. Materially assisting this situation was the 10th TRG, whose three squadrons had occupied Giramont, France, in late November. Reconnaissance of the 'bulge', an area which taken to all points of the compass actually covered 10,000 square miles, was vital in those desperate weeks.

On 17 December the 10th TRG's Mustangs laid on a maximum effort over Patton's Third Army front, and surprised enemy aircraft. In the afternoon three separate air battles developed in which seven German machines were downed by aircraft

of the 12th and 15th FSs. The first Bf 109 was shot down by 13-kill ace Clyde East, but the best score of the day fell to John Hoefker, who claimed three fighters plus a shared Ju 88, the latter having unwisely appeared on the scene. Following his successes Hoefker's tally had risen to 7.5 victories, thus making him the first recon ace in the ETO.

On the 19th, Clyde East was almost shot down by his wingman, Lt Henry Lacey, who fortunately got the Bf 109 which was trailing closely behind him – 'too close', as East succinctly wrote in his combat report. So bad had the weather conditions become that on 21 December, single-ship 'volunteer only' sorties were flown in order to give Allied troops some idea of where the Germans were and in what strength. Pilots like 'Blackie' Travis had to contend with the prevailing 50 ft ceiling and 100-yard visibility to obtain the data required.

Christmas 1944 saw the recon squadrons undertaking 'business as usual', and the 10th TRG was joined by the 160th and 161st Tac/R squadrons of the 363rd FG on 23 December – two pilots from the group shot down an Fw 190 on this date, but a pair of F-6s from the 15th TRS were lost the following day.

By late January conditions were still bad, but the offensive was at last able to move into higher gear, with a Rhine crossing taking top priority. In February the Ninth's fighters encountered German jets for the first time, two Me 262s attacking a squadron from the 354th while it was bombing Zellingen on the 17th. Both German machines were damaged in the ensuing melée, but no P-51s were lost. In common with most Groups, the formerly P-38-equipped 370th finished its war flying Mustangs on ground-attack missions, and although a number of aerial combats took place before VE-Day, pilots had little opportunity to add to their scores while flying the P-51D.

Although not a fighter ace, Capt 'Blackie' Travis was no less a hero following his extraordinary series of low-level flights in appalling snow blizzards during the height of the German breakout in the Ardennes in late December 1944. A member of the 12th TRS, Travis was one of a small band of pilots who volunteered to fly in conditions that saw the bulk of the Allied air forces grounded. Due to his bravery, Allied commanders managed to restore contact with several besieged battalions of US troops holding out against the German armoured thrust. Travis is seen here with his crew chief, SSgt 'Monk' Davidson, and his personally decorated F-6C, *MAZIE, ME AND MONK*, after the Battle of the Bulge had been won (*Davidson* via *Ivie*)

The tactical recon force flew a mix of F-6A, B, C and D model photo-Mustangs throughout its time in the ETO. And, as this late 1944 photograph of 42-103005 (F-6B of the 111th TRS) clearly shows, these units eventually adopted more standardised markings in line with other USAAF Groups, the code 'N5' identifying the 111th as one of three squadrons within the 69th TRG. In addition, green diagonal tail stripes were applied for a relatively brief period (*Olmsted*)

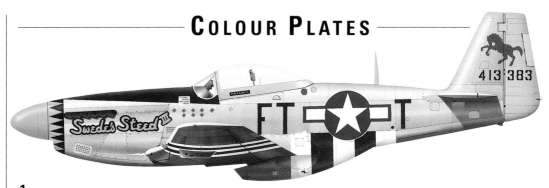

1
P-51D-5-NA (NA.109) 44-13383 *Swede's Steed III*, flown by 1st Lt William Y 'Swede' Anderson, 353rd FS/354th FG, Ninth Air Force

2
P-51B-1-NA (NA.102) 43-12375 *BONNIE "B" II*, flown by Capt Donald M 'Buzz' Beerbower, 353rd FS/354th FG, Ninth Air Force

3
P-51D-5-NA (NA.109) 44-13628 *BONNIE B III*, flown by Capt Donald M 'Buzz' Beerbower, CO 353rd FS/354th FG, Ninth Air Force

4
P-51D-5-NA (NA.109) 44-13693 *Angel's Playmate*, flown by Capt Bruce W Carr, 353rd FS/354th FG, Ninth Air Force

5
P-51B-10-NA (NA.104) 42-106602 *SHELLELAGH*, flown by Capt Kenneth H Dahlberg, 353rd FS/354th FG, Ninth Air Force

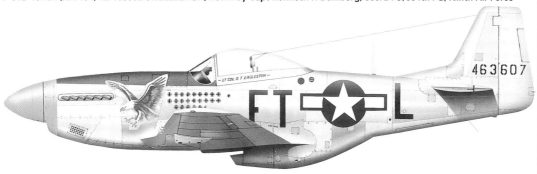

6
P-51D-20-NA (NA.122) 44-63607, flown by Lt Col Glenn T Eagleston, CO 353rd FS/354th FG, Ninth Air Force

7
P-51B-7-NA (NA.104) 43-6833 *Beantown Banshee*, flown by Capt Felix M Rogers, 353rd FS/354th FG, Ninth Air Force

8
P-51B-1-NA (NA.102) 43-12173 *"Peg O'my Heart"*, flown by 1st Lt George Bickell, 355th FS/354th FG, Ninth Air Force

9
P-51D-20-NA (NA.122) 44-63702 *"Grim Reaper"*, flown by Capt Lowell K Brueland, 355th FS/354th FG, Ninth Air Force

10
P-51B-1-NA (NA.102) 43-12451 *LIVE BAIT*, flown by Capt Clayton Gross, 355th FS/354th FG, Ninth Air Force

10A
P-51B-5-NA (NA.104) 43-6764 *Suga'*, flown by Capt Charles W Lasko, 355th FS/354th FG, Ninth Air Force

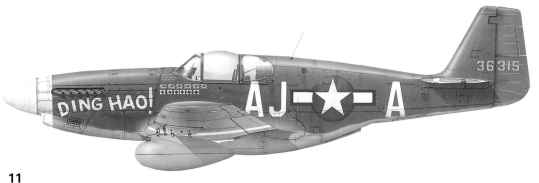

11
P-51B-5-NA (NA.104) 43-6315 *DING HAO!*, flown by Maj James Howard, CO 356th FS/354th FG, Ninth Air Force

12
P-51D-5-NA (NA.109) 44-13882 *UNO-WHO?*, flown by Maj George 'Max' Lamb, 356th FS/354th FG, Ninth Air Force

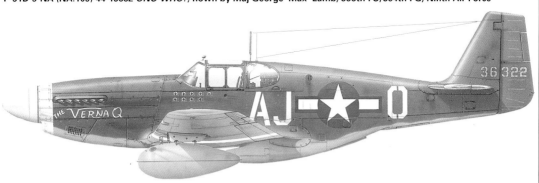

13
P-51B-5-NA (NA.104) 43-6322 *THE VERNA Q*, flown by Maj Frank O'Connor, 356th FS/354th FG, Ninth Air Force

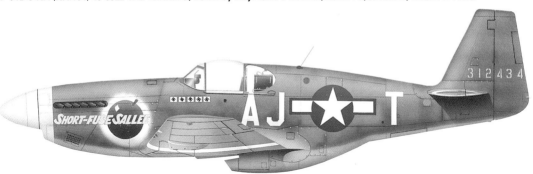

14
P-51B-I-NA (NA.102) 43-12434 *SHORT-FUSE SALLEE*, flown by Capt Richard Turner, 356th FS/354th FG, Ninth Air Force

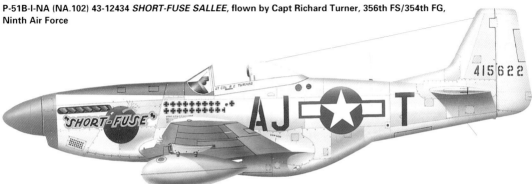

15
P-51D-15-NA (NA.109) 44-15622 "SHORT-FUSE", flown by Lt Col Richard Turner, CO 356th FS/354th FG, Ninth Air Force

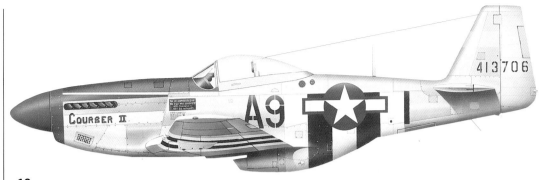

16
P-51D-5-NA (NA.109) 44-13706 *COURSER II*, flown by Capt Morton A Kammerlohr, 380th FS/363rd FG, Ninth Air Force

17
P-51B-10-NA (NA.104) 42-106486 *Virginia*, flown by Robert McGee, 382nd FS/363rd FG, Ninth Air Force

18
P-51B-5-NA (NA.104) 43-6438, *HOO FLUNG DUNG*, flown by Maj Robert McWherter, 382nd FS/363rd FG, Ninth Air Force

19
P-51D-5-NA (NA.109) 44-13380, *HOO FLUNG DUNG*, flown by Maj Robert McWherter, 382nd FS/363rd FG, Ninth Air Force

20
P-51D-20-NA (NA.122) 44-63675, *Sierra Sue II*, flown by Robert Bohna, 402nd FS/370th FG, Ninth Air Force

21
P-51D-20-NA (NA.122) 44-63819 *KEEP SMILIN'*, flown by Charles Nelson, 402nd FS/370th FG, Ninth Air Force

22
F-6D, ex-P-51D-10-NA (NA.109) 44-14306 *Lil' Margaret*, flown by Capt Clyde B East, 15th TRS/10th PRG, Ninth Air Force

23
F-6CNT ex-P-51C-5-NT 42-103368, flown by Capt John Hoefker, 15th TRS/10th PRG, Ninth Air Force

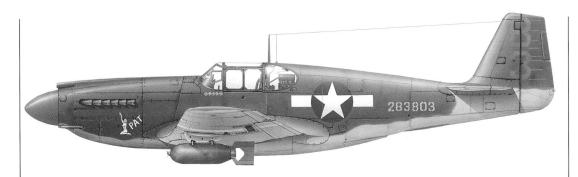

24
A-36A-1-NA (NA.97) 42-83803 *PAT*, flown by Lt Michael T Russo, 522nd FBS/27th FBG, Twelfth Air Force

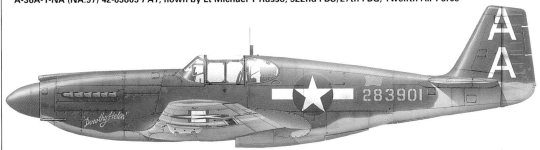

25
A-36A-1-NA (NA.97) 42-83901 *"Dorothy Helen"*, flown by John P Crowder, 524th FBS/27th FBG, Twelfth Air Force

26
P-51B-10-NA (NA.104) 42-106511, flown by Col Charles M McCorkle, CO 31st FG, Fifteenth Air Force

27
P-51D sub-type and serial unknown *Tempus Fugit*, flown by Col Bill Daniel, CO 31st FG, Fifteenth Air Force

28
P-51D-5-NA (NA.109) 44-13382 *February*, flown by Lt James Brooks, 307th FS/31st FG, Fifteenth Air Force

29
P-51D-5-NA (NA.109) 44-13464, flown by Maj Sam Brown, CO 307th FS/31st FG, Fifteenth Air Force

30
P-51D-5-NA (NA.109) 44-13500 *Flying DUTCHMAN*, flown by Capt Robert Goebel, 308th FS/31st FG, Fifteenth Air Force

31
P-51D-5-NA (NA.109) 44-13494 *"MISS MIMI II"*, flown by Capt Walter J Goehausen, Jr, 308th FS/31st FG, Fifteenth Air

32
P-51D-5-NA (NA.109) 44-13311 *OKaye*, flown by Maj Leland P Molland, CO 308th FS/31st FG, Fifteenth Air Force

33
P-51D-15-NA (NA.109) 44-15459 *AMERICAN BEAUTY*, flown by Capt John Voll, 308th FS/31st FG, Fifteenth Air Force

34
P-51D-25-NA (NA.124) 44-72777, flown by Maj Ralph J 'Doc' Watson, Operations Officer, 52nd FG, Fifteenth Air Force

35
P-51C-5-NT (NA.103) 42-103579 *Julie*, flown by Lt Robert Curtis, 2nd FS/52nd FG, Fifteenth Air Force

36
P-51D-5-NA (NA.109) 44-13298 *"Marie"*, flown by Capt Freddie F Ohr, 2nd FS/52nd FG, Fifteenth Air Force

37
P-51C-5-NT (NA.103) 42-103582, flown by Lt Calvin D Allen, Jr, 5th FS/52nd FG, Fifteenth Air Force

38
P-51B-15-NA (NA.104) 43-24853 *Little Ambassador*, flown by Lt James W Empey, 5th FS/52nd FG, Fifteenth Air Force

39
P-51C-10-NT (NA.103) 42-103867 *SHIMMY III*, flown by Lt Col Chester L Sluder, CO 325th FG, Fifteenth Air Force

40
P-51D-5-NA (NA.109) 44-13483 *LITTLE STUD,* flown by Col Robert L Baseler, CO 325th FG, Fifteenth Air Force

41
P-51D-5-NA (NA.109) 44-13299 *THISIZIT,* flown by Capt Richard W Dunkin, 317th FS/325th FG, Fifteenth Air Force

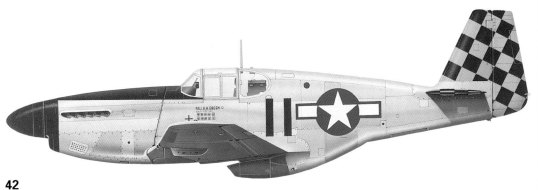

42
P-51C-I-NT (NA.103) 42-103324, flown by Maj Herschel 'Herky' Green, CO 317th FS/325th FG, Fifteenth Air Force

43
P-51D-5-NA (NA.109) 44-13440 *Ballzout II,* flown by Lt Walter R Hinton, 317th FS/325th FG, Fifteenth Air Force

44
P-51B-15-NA (NA.104) 43-24877 *Penrod*, flown by Capt Roy B Hogg, CO 318th FS/325th FG, Fifteenth Air Force

45
P-51D-10-NA (NA.109) 44-14467 *MARY MAC*, flown by Lt Gordon H McDaniel, 318th FS/325th FG, Fifteenth Air Force

46
P-51D-20-NA 44-63512 *SHU SHU*, flown by Maj Norman L McDonald, CO 318th FS/325th FG, Fifteenth Air Force

47
P-51B-15-NA (NA.104) 43-24857 *Dorothy-II*, flown by Capt Robert M Barkey, 319th FS/325th FG, Fifteenth Air Force

48
P-51B/C sub-type and serial unknown *TOPPER III*, flown by Capt Ed Toppins, 99th FS/332nd FG, Fifteenth Air Force

49
P-51 D-15-NA (NA.109) 44-15569 *BUNNIE*, flown by Capt Roscoe C Brown, CO 100th FS/332nd FG, Fifteenth Air Force

50
P-51C-5-NT (NA.103) serial unknown *Miss-Pelt*, flown by Lt Clarence 'Lucky' Lester, 100th FS/332nd FG, Fifteenth Air Force

51
P-51D sub-type and serial unknown *Creamer's Dream*, flown by Lt Charles White, 301st FS/332nd FG, Fifteenth Air Force

52
P-51C-10-NT (NA.111) serial unknown *"INA The MACON BELLE"*, flown by Lt Lee 'Buddy' Archer, 302nd FS/332nd FG,
Fifteenth Air Force

53
P-51D sub-type and serial unknown *"Little Freddie"*, flown by Lt Freddie Hutchins, 302nd FS/332nd FG, Fifteenth Air Force

54
Mustang Mk III FZ152, flown by Wg Cdr Stanislaw Skalski, OC No 133 Wg, RAF

55
Mustang Mk III FB201, flown by Flg Off B M Vassiliades, No 19 Sqn, RAF

56
Mustang Mk III FZ120, flown by Sqn Ldr Derrick Westenra, OC No 65 Sqn, RAF

57
Mustang Mk III FB309, flown by Flt Lt Raymond V Hearn, No 112 Sqn, RAF

58
Mustang Mk III FZ149, flown by Flt Sgt W Nowoczyn, No 306 *Torunski* Sqn, RAF

59
Mustang Mk III FB387, flown by Sqn Ldr Eugeniusz Horbaczewski, OC No 315 *Deblinski* Sqn, RAF

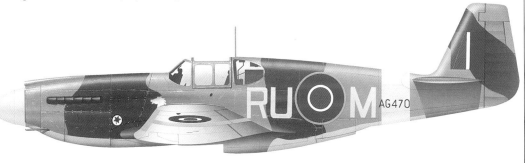

60
Mustang Mk I AG470, flown by Flg Off Hollis Hills, No 414 Sqn, RCAF

1
Lt Wendell O Pruitt of the 302nd
FS/332nd FG is seen in mid-1944

2
Pruitt's 'side-kick' in the air was Lt Lee
'Buddy' Archer, also of the 302nd FS

3
Lt Col Glenn T Eagleston, CO of the
353rd FS/354th FG in 1945

4
Lt Bruce W Carr of the 353rd FS/354th
FG is seen in mid-April 1945

5
Flg Off Hollis H Hills of No 414 Sqn,
RCAF, as he appeared in August 1942

6
Maj Robert C McWherter was the
363rd FG's top scoring pilot

RAF MUSTANGS IN NORTH AFRICA AND ITALY

Although the Mustang Mk III was to predominate in RAF squadrons towards the end of the campaign in North Africa and Italy, some of the first examples of the Mustang line to bear British markings in that theatre of war were in fact Mk IIs of No 225 Sqn, the unit having initially flown Mk Is on Tac/R duties from Thruxton in May 1942, prior to heading overseas. These aircraft were used until October when the squadron moved to North Africa, apparently leaving the Mustangs behind. Based as Maison Blanche, with detachments at Bone, No 225 continued in the reconnaissance role by utilising a handful of surplus USAAF P-51s until July 1943, when these weary aircraft were finally replaced by Spitfire Mk VCs

In addition, No 14 Sqn, which otherwise operated Marauders, received a number of Mk Is in May 1943, although they were gone by the following month. No 1437 Strategic Reconnaissance Flight also flew the type on Tac/R sorties before the invasion of Italy. Once the Allies were established ashore, they were able to base aircraft in the southern part of the country, and moves were made to re-equip a number of Desert Air Force (DAF) squadrons with Mk IIIs. All these units had previously flown the Warhawk/Kittyhawk on fighter-bomber duties, and in the main the Mustangs undertook a similar role.

Continuing as part of the DAF's excellent support of the British Eighth Army was No 239 Wg with four Kittyhawk squadrons – Nos 3 (RAAF),

One of six A-36A Invaders (probably 42-84019) used by No 1437 Strategic Reconnaissance Flight, and flown initially with British national insignia and single letter ID codes. By the time this photograph was taken at Foggia, in Italy, on 18 November 1943, British serial numbers (HK944 in this case) had replaced the rear-fuselage AAF serial. When No 1437 Flt disbanded in October, this aircraft passed to No 260 Sqn for non-operational training. Note the gas detection patches positioned forward of the wing leading edge and on the fuselage spine (*H Levy*)

Having set something of a wartime trend by painting the much admired, and copied, 'sharkmouth' on its Desert Air Force Warhawks, No 112 Sqn continued with the tradition on its Mustang Mk IIIs and IVs. One of the former, FB290, is seen here in typically spartan surroundings. The aircraft subsequently served with Nos 260 and 3 RAAF Sqns before being destroyed by flak on 3 April 1945 whilst operating with the latter unit. It appears that few Malcolm canopies were supplied with the Mk IIIs destined for service in the Middle East

5 (SAAF) and 112 and 260 (RAF). Of these No 260 received its first Mustang Mk IIIs in April, with No 112 converting in June, No 5 in September and No 3 in November.

Commanded by Australian Gp Capt Brian Eaton, No 239 Wg was kept busy not only supporting the Allied armies in Italy, but mounting long-range strikes across the other side of the Adriatic to materially assist Yugoslavian partisans – assistance that was to culminate in formation of the Balkan Air Force on 7 June. No 260 Sqn contributed the Mustang element of this force, under the control of No 283 Wg.

Luftwaffe activity was sporadic as the ground war progressed slowly up the Italian 'boot' – by 5 June 1944, when Rome was liberated, the Luftwaffe fighter force had almost entirely withdrawn to leave defence of the country in the capable hands of the Italian fascist air force, the RSI, equipped with a mix of Bf 109Gs and modern Italian fighters like the Fiat G.55 and Macchi C.202/205V.

All these types were a close match for the Mustang Mk III, but in general the appearance of enemy aircraft did not disrupt support operations to a great extent. As was so often the case elsewhere, the biggest hazard to fighter-bombers was small arms and AA fire. Flying combat missions over the Italian front and the Balkans No 5 SAAF, based at Fano on the Adriatic coast, was invariably busy. Its Mustangs flew strafing, or 'Pig', sorties interspersed with bombing missions and escort to USAAF B-25s and South African Venturas, Liberators and PR Mosquitos. Railways provided many targets including bridges, marshalling yards and rolling stock as the Germans sought to hold territory under increasing pressure.

It was over Italy that the 'cab rank' system of *Rover Joe* air support, utilising an airborne forward air controller flying an Auster or Piper Cub, was developed to a high degreee. No 5 Sqn SAAF was among the Mustang

Mustang Mk III of No 250 'Sudan' Sqn, No 239 Wg, undergoes some fairly extensive attention while based in Italy during the last weeks of the war. At the end of lengthy supply lines, both RAF and USAAF units in the Mediterranean were not over-burdened with ground support equipment, as the ubiquitous oil drum, which served many purposes outside of being a mere container, well illustrates (*Arthur Cotton*)

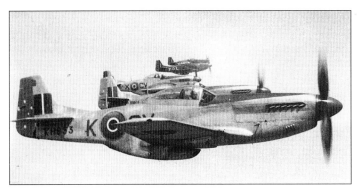

The Mustang Mk IVs of No 3 Sqn RAAF were operated in both camouflage and natural metal, the unit's aircraft sporting mid-blue rudders with the Southern Cross celestial body superimposed. This formation is led by KH853 'CV-K', which had initially served with No 260 Sqn before passing to the Australian unit

Another No 3 Sqn RAAF Mk IV – this machine also boasts the bright (by RAF standards at least) markings used by the unit, although in this particular case the codes were applied in the same shade of blue as used on the rudder. As with most fighter units in Italy late in 1945, No 3 Sqn was predominantly engaged in ground attack sorties, with bombs being carried on many missions

units operating in the region which was able to exploit this invaluable and highly successful assistance given to tactical operations. Co-ordinating their observations with a ground controller (who was usually an experienced fighter-bomber pilot), fully armed Mustangs and 'Kitty-bombers' patrolled the battle area until called in on a target. Attacks would be carried out with guns, 500 or 1000-lb bombs and, towards the end of 1944, rocket projectiles. The performance penalty imposed on the Mustang by the cumbersome launch rails had prevented Mk IIIs from operating with this weapon in the more heavily-contested skies of Western Europe, but Axis air power in Italy was such that there was relatively little risk of Mustang Mk III pilots encountering any aerial opposition.

Just to prove the exception to the rule, however, the Balkan Air Force ran into the Luftwaffe on 14 July when No 213 Sqn came across a dozen Hs 126s, escorted by seven Bf 109s, and swiftly shot down two of each air-craft type.

By late 1944 277 Mk IIIs had been delivered to RAF squadrons of the Mediterranean Allied Air Forces, together with 46 Mk IVs. As in Europe the Mk IV – incidentally referred to by its American designation of P-51D/P-51K at least within No 239 Wg, probably in order to differentiate it from the Mk III – was introduced to maintain operational require-ments, both marks being used concurrently.

Despite the healthy number of aircraft delivered from the UK, Mus-tang attrition and losses to ground fire had been high and No 213 Sqn was forced to take over No 249 Sqn's Mk IIIs on 14 April 1944, the latter receiving Spitfire Mk IXs in their place. These were used on long-range patrols and armed reconnaissance sweeps across the Adriatic, as well as tactical recce sorties for the Fifteenth AAF, and from August its aircraft began carrying bombs for ground-attack work. This remained No 213's primary operational duty until the war ended, by which time Mustang IVs had been part of the inventory for some three months.

No 213 Sqn had built up a considerable tally of air victories since its days as a fighter squadron in the UK and Middle East, and the Mustang Mk III enabled this to be steadily increased in the last year of the war – the unit constantly encountered the enemy over Yugoslavia and Albania during sweeps performed as part of No 283 Wg based at Biferno, on the Adriatic coast. No 213 Sqn finished the war with over 200 confirmed kills to its credit, the majority of this score having been achieved in 1940/41.

Also based at Fano was No 3 Sqn

RAAF, which experienced the common slackening of pace in air operations as the winter of 1944/45 brought bad weather with low cloud to increase the normal hazards of operational flying. Pilots were easily lost or simply went missing in such conditions, and there were numerous sortie cancellations until the conditions improved – it was foolhardy to risk men and machines unnecessarily. Axis fight-

ers generally made little impression, but a flight of Australian Mustangs was nevertheless bounced by two Bf 109Gs on 26 December 1944. One Mk III was shot down and in reply one of the enemy fighters was damaged when Sqn Ldr Murray Nash and Flg Offs Andrews and Thomas waded in to drive off the Messerschmitts.

As the dire German position resulted in increasing Allied gains, there were some sorties which were out of the ordinary for the pilots, one such mission being the No 239 Wg attack on Venice on 21 March. Extreme precision was called for to avoid damaging the ancient city's priceless art treasures as RAF Mustangs co-ordinated their strikes with those of 79th FG Thunderbolts to destroy Axis shipping in Venice Harbour. In the event the fighter-bombers dropped all but a single bomb in the harbour area, one Mustang hitting the Palazzo Quay. So accurate was the attack that the Venetians turned out to watch!

With German resistance in northern Italy finally crumbling by late April the ground troops made significant progress in a campaign that had been long and costly. To hasten the German retreat came the last round of Allied air strikes, and the last operation for Italian-based RAF Mustangs, which took place on 6 May – sadly, five days prior to this last Mustang action No 5 Sqn SAAF had suffered the loss of its OC, Maj H Clarke, whose aircraft had crashed into the Adriatic between Trieste and Grado while attacking shipping.

Complete with a large Desert Air Force badge, this Mustang Mk IV of No 112 Sqn carried the name *Marisa* on the canopy bar, and served as the personal mount of Wg Cdr (later Group Capt) Brian Eaton. His three-letter initial 'BAE' was applied diagonally below the cockpit to complete a very striking, and suitably different, paint scheme

Another view of Gp Capt Ross-Shore's Mk IV KM182, seen here parked on the line in Italy with its lower engine cowls off immediately after the war – clearly visible are the in-situ tie-down ropes, which were very important if the flightline was subjected to high winds. It didn't take much for the rudder of an unfettered fighter to act like a sail and shove it into its neighbour, which could result at best in minor dents and fabric tears that could nevertheless stop the aircraft from flying on the next operation (*Arthur Cotton*)

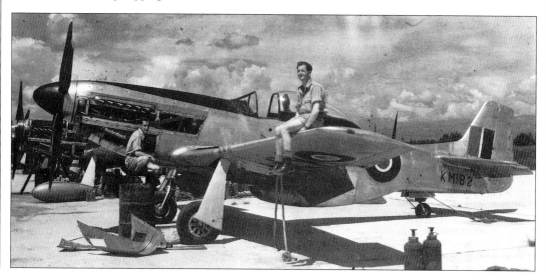

AMERICAN 'STUKA'

The distinction of being the first Mustangs to see operational service with the US Army rests with the 35 P-51-2NA (later designated F-6As) shipped to North Africa via the UK in the spring of 1943. These machines, configured similarly to RAF Tac Recon Mustangs, were introduced into action by the 154th Observation Squadron of the 68th Observation Group during April. Some of the new aircraft found their way to the 111th, which shared the base at Oujda in French Morocco. The 68th operated a variety of aircraft on tactical reconnaissance and photographic sorties, whilst after only a few weeks the 154th was withdrawn from combat and transferred to training duties, its aircraft passing to the 111th TRS in time to participate in operations over Sicily.

Nicknamed 'The Snoopers', the 111th TRS, which became the only USAAF unit of its kind in North Africa, soldiered on with its P-51As until they were largely replaced by P-51Cs (F-6Cs) during the spring of 1944 – a necessary move as the supply of A-models had by that time all but dried up.

INVADER DIVE-BOMBERS

As mentioned earlier, the AAF ordered 500 examples of the NA-73, designated the A-36A, and these reached Stateside training units by spring 1942. While the US Army had long had a tradition of including attack bombers in its inventory, the number of types specifically designed as dive-bombers were relatively few. Aiming the aircraft at the target prior to bomb release remained, however, a reliable method of aerial destruction which at best offered greater accuracy than conventional bombing against small targets. Much impressed with the Luftwaffe's deployment of the Ju 87 in the early stages of the war, Army chiefs decreed that the A-36A would undertake a similar role.

The third P-51 built (41-37322) passed to the 154th Observation Squadron to be named *MAH SWEET Eva Lee*, presumably by the pilot, Lt N F Bush, whose name it carried on 25 June 1943 when photographed at Hergla, Tunisia. These early Mustangs clocked up hundreds of PR sorties. The US flag on the tail is a carry-over from the Operation *Torch* landings in French North Africa, when 'Old Glory' seemed the most appropriate way to identify American aircraft in the MTO. Note the bulged window behind the cockpit where the camera was installed (*H Levy*)

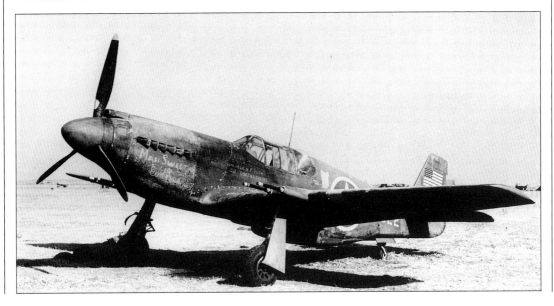

Accordingly, the aircraft was fitted with wing dive-brakes and stressed to withstand the forces imposed on the airframe when the aircraft was put into a steep dive under full power. North American built a good deal of strength into the NA-73 airframe, and the A-36 proved well able to carry out this exacting task. Pilots, on the other hand, initially found dive-bombing difficult to master, and there were many accidents during training. The programme was nevertheless pressed ahead with, and two groups – the 27th and 86th Bombardment Groups (L) – were assigned to the Twelfth Air Force to use the A-36 in action in North Africa. The 86th was the first to go overseas in March 1943.

About 300 A-36As were available in North Africa by late May, and the following month the 27th, under Lt Col John Stevenson, made its debut as a dive-bomber outfit, flying combat missions against the island of Pantelleria as a prelude to the invasion of Sicily.

It was the general Allied progress against the Germans in the Mediterranean that prompted a name for the A-36. Lt Robert B Walsh of the 27th suggested, 'Why don't we call them Invaders, since we're always invading places?' He had a point, and 'Invader' the A-36A became, at least until early 1944 by which time 'Mustang' was in more general use for the North American fighter – this name was never applied to the A-36A.

As was not unknown in other cases, Stateside training difficulties belied the success of the A-36 in combat. Both frontline groups developed reliable techniques to exploit the aircraft's strength and good low altitude performance, these attributes being adaptable to handle different combat situations and a variety of targets. By keeping very much to the original concept of dive-bombing, the 27th BG found that diving at 90° from around 8000 ft, with each aircraft armed with two 500-lb bombs, proved to be extremely effective. Deploying the two-foot wide segmented wing dive-brakes reduced airspeed to about 390 mph.

Each A-36 peeled off and adopted a follow-the-leader dive, maintaining about 150 ft separation; as deploying the dive-brakes reduced each aircraft to much the same speed, they were always close. It was not uncommon for 20 of them to be in the dive at the same time, and the sound they made was incredible. Eye-witnesses confirmed that the Ju 87 Stuka had nothing on the scream of a squadron of Invaders! The downside was that German flak gunners often had little difficulty in tracking the hurtling fighter-bombers, and the main casualties the 27th and 86th suffered were to groundfire.

Neither did the Luftwaffe and Regia Aeronautica ignore the Amer-

This A-36A Invader wears the early markings of the 27th FBG, Twelfth Air Force, at Hergla, Tunisia, on 13 June 1943. The letter 'A' almost certainly indicated the 524th FBS, with 'V' being the individual aircraft letter. The 27th (and 86th) were unique for not only being among the few to operate the Invader in the dive-bombing role, but also because such land-based squadrons were soon to pass out of the inventory of almost every air arm the world over (*H Levy*)

The final unit markings worn by Invaders of the 27th FBG consisted of a two-letter code applied in the style shown in this line up of aircraft of the 523rd FBS, with 42-83987/'CX' nearest the camera, and 42-83996/'CB' sitting alongside. Both aircraft have bomb logs, a common marking within Twelfth Air Force dive-bomber squadrons, with some individual aircraft recording scores of over 100 sorties (*via Mackay*)

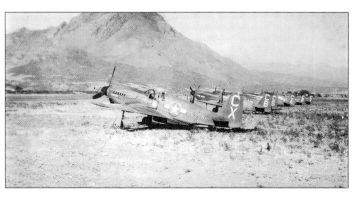

A P-51 in the typically anonymous markings which manifested the early period of USAAF operations in the MTO. Invaders and Mustangs were never strikingly marked as there was little tactical need at the time, but the theatre bands in yellow, plus a red spinner, were universally applied to assist recognition (*via Mackay*)

Surrounded by its groundcrew, battle-seasoned A-36A *Margie H* was the personal aircraft of Capt Lawrence Dye, who flew with the 522nd FBS in Tunisia in 1943. As is clearly visible on the aircraft's nose, Dye was not adverse to a little aerial combat after he had delivered his bombs. The memory of this Invader lives on today as the USAF Museum's A-36 (the only surviving example in the world) is painted up in this scheme and displayed at Wright-Patterson AFB in Ohio (*AFM via Ivie*)

ican dive-bombers, and although enemy fighters were not a significant factor in the Invaders' war, pilots did score aerial kills. The 27th BG's Lt Michael T Russo of the 522nd FBS made ace while flying the A-36A, leading all other pilots of the two groups in terms of victories. His first damaged claim was an Fw 190 *Jabo* caught in the act of bombing Allied shipping off Salerno on 13 September 1943. Twelve '190s were observed by 'Red' and 'White' flights of the squadron, and after dropping their bombs the German fighters split up and dived down to wave height. Russo caught up with one and managed just a single short burst, observing hits, but he did not see the aircraft crash.

A further damaged claim on an Fw 190 was filed by Russo the following day, and it was 24 October before he claimed a confirmed victory – a Fieseler Storch, mistakenly identified as a biplane in his combat report. Russo was on a bombing mission to Avezzano on 8 December when he noticed an airfield north of the town. Carrying out a strafing attack, he observed three Ju 52s about to become airborne. One took off and a long burst from the A-36's guns hit the transport, which was less than 60 ft off the ground. It promptly exploded and crashed.

On 30 December Russo nailed a Bf 109G in the Rome area during a routine bombing sortie. He had observed a pair of Messerschmitts attempting to intercept his formation from the port side, so had broken away from his flight. Russo then saw two more Bf 109Gs away to starboard, and turning in that direction closed up and fired a short burst of tracer. The enemy pilot pulled up as if to bail out, but the Messerschmitt went out of control and into a spin from which it did not recover.

Although more often than not A-36 pilots completed their tour of duty without even seeing an enemy aircraft, let alone shooting one down, the four squadrons of the 27th achieved a total of 53 enemy aircraft confirmed destroyed. Michael Russo's five must have been an inspiration as his squadron claimed the most with 30. This highly respectable score for what was first and foremost an attack outfit, was the source of much pride in a group which would have placed combating the Luftwaffe some way down its list of operational priorities.

The 27th and 86th were redesignated as fighter-bomber groups in September 1943 (the former on the 11th), and each was reduced from four to three component squadrons – a move which enabled the heavy losses to be absorbed for the time being. At Salerno the A-36's 30-

minute loiter time made it much in demand as its ability to stay around and hit targets of opportunity was better than any Allied fighter in-theatre. Consequently, the 27th and 86th were called upon to undertake strafing, escort and glide-bombing attacks, which considerably reduced the number of casualties suffered to flak when compared with diving steeply on the target.

By the autumn of 1943 replacements were becoming critical as the 111th TRS received A-36s to make good the losses of P-51As – by this stage in the war neither of the two early model Mustangs remained in production. The writing was on the wall by early 1944 when the 27th passed its remaining A-36As to the 86th and converted to P-40 Warhawks, and later still P-47s. In its turn the 86th also received P-47s, and the surviving battle-weary A-36s passed to training units – a final step before being scrapped.

─────── ENTER THE FIFTEENTH ───────

On 1 November 1943 the Twelfth Air Force was split into two components on the activation of a new strategic bombing force, the Fifteenth Air Force. No time was lost in initiating bombing missions under the *Pointblank* Directive as B-17s attacked the La Spezia naval base on the day the Fifteenth was activated. Initially concerned with building up a strong force of bombers to hit targets that were out of reach of the Eighth Air Force in England, the Fifteenth continued to rely on units assigned to the Twelfth Air Force for fighter escort for the time being.

Earlier campaigns had established a separate Mediterranean Theatre of Operations (MTO) as a generic combat area stretching from North Africa, via Sicily and Corsica, and ultimately encompassing Italy and large chunks of southern Europe. Fighter pilots assigned to MTO units found that instead of the 200+ hours they would have been required to fly before rotation in the ETO, their tour of duty was now at least 300 hours.

With the Allies established in Italy the bombers occupied eight airfields on the Foggia plain, said to be large enough to 'base all the air forces in all the world'. Soon fighters, heavy bombers, mediums, liaison types and transports came in to cram the Foggia complex of airfields which was fortunately never subjected to a German air attack serious enough to disrupt operations for any length of time – the weather would achieve that all too frequently. Disappointingly, in view of the anticipated conditions actually being an improvement on those experienced by the Eighth in England, the Fifteenth Air Force would not at times be able to achieve the kind of dual knockout punch eagerly sought by AAF chiefs solely due to 'natural causes'.

At full strength, a mixed line of 52nd FG P-51Cs and Ds await the signal to taxy out on the PSP ready to form up for take-off. The aircraft in the foreground was the regular mount of the 5th FS's joint leading ace, Lt Calvin D Allen, Jr, who scored 7 kills during his MTO/ETO tour. Unlike most UK-based groups, who transitioned quickly from B and Cs to Ds as soon as the 'bubble-tops' became available, the Mustang squadrons in Italy flew a mix of types well into the autumn of 1944 (*Murphey via Ivie*)

On 1 April 1944 the Twelfth Air Force's two Spitfire groups, the 31st and 52nd, were transferred to Fifteenth AF control prior to both converting to P-51Bs. On 21 April the 31st provided 36 P-51s as escorts for a bombing raid on Ploesti, Rumania, and came home with claims of 17-7-10. The enemy fighters' targets were the B-24s

which had not apparently received a recall order, and the P-51 pilots had a tough fight on their hands. Two Mustangs were lost in the series of dog-fights that ensued, but the impressive score resulted in the first of the Group's two Distinguished Unit Citations being awarded during this period.

The transfer of the 31st and 52nd FGs to the operational control of the Fifteenth was followed in May by that of the all-Negro-manned 332nd (which initially retained its P-47s prior to converting to P-51Cs in June) and 325th FGs. All fighter units thus came under the control of the 306th Fighter Wing, the Mustangs joining three existing P-38 groups.

Aviation Engineer battalions had their work cut out to provide suitable bases for air operations from Italy. Many airfields had been subjected to Allied bombing and the Germans had left few buildings or other facilities intact for the new occupiers. A general shortage of wood hampered the construction of suitable accommodation for pilots and groundcrews, and for months many airfields maintained a scruffy 'half-finished' appearance. Priority was naturally given to maintaining runways and dispersal areas, both of which required vast quantities of pierced steel planking (PSP) as seasonal changes brought extremes of heat and heavy rain to wash away impacted earth, sand or rubble foundations, thus creating uneven surfaces that could play havoc with aircraft tyres. Throughout the campaign the airfield construction gangs, assisted by local labour, more than earned their pay in Italy.

Having had its pilots fly Spitfires down to North Africa and return in P-51s, the 52nd FG occupied Ghisonaccia, a new base which became a disagreeable 'dust-bowl' on every take-off; some compensation came in the form of ex-'Eagle' Squadron ace Maj James Goodson, now of the 4th FG, who had arrived on 12 April to oversee the new groups' safe transition to the P-51. Goodson's reputation had preceded him, and both the 31st and 52nd appreciated his help in making the change-over from Spit-fire to Mustang as trouble-free as possible, and thus ensuring the minimum loss of operational efficiency. During his month-long stay he flew several sorties, claiming a pair of Bf 109Gs during a bombing raid to Wiener-Neustadt, in Austria, on 23 April. On 14 May the 52nd moved to Madna, lying to the south of Termoli on the Adriatic and on the 18th

As the Mediterranean developed into a major war theatre, depots were established to handle the influx of aircraft that arrived by sea, crated and disassembled. This view of part of the 36th Air Depot at Maison Blanche, Algeria, taken in April 1944 shows P-51Bs in final assembly, a process which included applying the yellow band theatre markings to the wings (*USAF*)

flew its first P-51 escort mission when it accompanied B-17s on a raid to the notorious oil refinery complex at Ploesti.

At that time, the 31st FG operated from San Severo, the 332nd from Ramitelli and the 325th from Lesina. On 12 May a milestone mission for the Fifteenth was the first 1000 bomber mission against a variety of Italian targets.

Further escort missions followed for the 52nd FG, and on 24 May

Capt Richard 'Dixie' Alexander made ace while covering B-24s bound for Linz, in Austria. Also flying with him in his section that day was the eventual second-ranking P-51 ace of the of the Fifteenth AAF, Capt James 'Sully' Varnell, Jr – his nickname 'Sully' was derived from Sullins, his middle name! Varnell had joined the 2nd FS of the 52nd in July 1943 after completing the short conversion syllabus at the North African Fighter Training Center on 30 June.

Just to prove that the P-51B's gun-jamming problem experienced by pilots of the Eighth AAF was not confined to the damp conditions of north-western Europe, Varnell suffered chronic stoppages during an escort mission flown on 16 June to Czechoslovakia. Taking his flight down to attack 55 enemy fighters preparing to hit the bombers, he did not let the odds, or his malfunctioning guns, cramp his style. Part of the official citation to his Silver Star award for this mission read:

'Lt Varnell destroyed two enemy fighters, assisted his flight in destroying two others and damaging another, while his squadron destroyed six others without loss or injury to themselves. Although his guns had jammed after his last encounter, Lt Varnell, despite such handicap, courageously dove on an enemy fighter that was attacking a lone bomber, forcing it to break off its attack.'

The seasoned 325th FG – already known as the 'Checkertail Clan' following their adoption of black and gold tail markings for their P-40 Warhawks almost a year earlier – received its first P-51Bs and Cs on 27 May. Then based at Lesina, Italy, some pilots had some reservations about trading P-47s for P-51s, but once a few basic facts of life were imparted, they grew both to appreciate the Mustang as well as to respect it. One of these lessons was to be very wary of the fact that the aircraft's centre of gravity could shift if violent manoeuvres were attempted with more than 15 gallons of fuel in the 85-gal capacity fuselage tank. Thrown into a spin or roll in that condition, the P-51 could bite, fatally.

The CO of the 325th's 317th FS unwittingly demonstrated this drawback (it was no more than that) by attempting a roll after a pull up from an on-the-deck pass. He never made it, having to hit the silk when the Mustang went into an inverted flat spin. Fortunately he survived, but it was an indelible lesson to both experienced aviators and the replacement 'hot rock' fighter jockeys who were assigned to the 'Checkertails' and other groups. Few of them ever took the P-51 for granted.

By the time the Mustang appeared in numbers in southern European

The 5th FS of the 52nd FG produced just four aces, with the pilot of this P-51B, Lt James W Empey, being the lowest scorer (5 kills) of this quartet. All his victories were claimed with this machine (43-24853), which he christened *Little Ambassador* (*Empey via Ivie*)

The man and his machine – Empey poses for an informal snapshot perched on the cockpit sill of his P-51B. His modestly decorated scoreboard (seen in the shot above) contrasted markedly with some of the more elaborate offerings from fellow aces within the Eighth and Ninth AAFs (*Empey via Ivie*)

skies, AAF pilots also realised what their colleagues in the Eighth and Ninth Air Forces could have told them – their P-51Bs and Cs looked far too much like the Bf 109 for comfort. By the spring of 1944 Mustang squadrons of the Fifteenth were likely to meet Germans, Italians and Rumanians in combat, not to mention fellow Americans whose aircraft recognition was occasionally in sore need of improvement. Bright group tail markings both enhanced espirit de corps and helped reduce

A formation shot of two 317th FS P-51D-5s taken in mid-1944 on a flight out of Lesina The lead aircraft, *The Lone Wolfe*, is flown by Lt Harold C Wolfe, and it carries four kill markings beneath the canopy (*Crow*)

the 'friend or foe?' problem, as did standard theatre recognition colours, but it was never entirely eliminated.

Things slowly improved when the early Mustangs eventually gave way to the P-51D, but as always much depended on there being time to note the unmistakable 'bubble' canopy which was this model's most outstanding recognition feature. Another factor in reducing 'friendly fire' incidents was the decreasing number of fighter sorties flown by the Luftwaffe.

Capt John Voll of the 31st FG's 308th FS was eventually to emerge as the Group's highest scorer, as well as finishing as the leading ace in the MTO. He joined the Group on 4 May 1944, and on the 14th flew his first mission over northern Italy, the general area where enemy fighters were then most likely to intercept the bombers. After learning his craft during a month of escort missions, Voll opened his score on 23 June over Ploesti.

On 29 May Maj Sam Brown and his wingman took on 50 enemy fighters over Sofia. Then commanding the 307th FS, Brown had previously served a tour in the Aleutians before being posted to the Mediterranean, and on this day his experience showed. Despite his Mustang having sustained serious damage, he caught up with the German fighters near Vienna and shot down three of them. Once back over friendly territory, Brown was forced to bail out of his P-51 when it caught fire.

Inspirational leader of the 31st FG, Col Charles 'Sandy' McCorkle (smiling, centre) conducts a pre-flight brief in front of his P-51B, *Betty Jane*, for the benefit of the USAAF photographer present. Four of the five pilots listening intently to their skipper's instructions are aces, and their details are as follows: from left to right, 2nd Lt Robert H Little (no recorded kills), 1st Lt Walter J Goehausen, Jr, (10 kills), Capt Leland P Molland (10.5 kills), Col McCorkle (11 kills), Capt Murray D McLaughlin (7 kills) and 2nd Lt John J Voll (21 kills) (*USAF*)

June was a good month for the Mustang pilots, and Ploesti was where the air action could be found, particularly for the 31st FG. Capt Robert Riddle of the 307th also scored during the Ploesti mission of the 23rd that saw Voll claim his first kill. Two enemy aircraft were credited to Riddle, plus a further pair damaged. Also successful on that same mission was Col Charles McCorkle of the 309th, who was Group CO at that time. His score of three downed and one damaged was a personal best. Nicknamed 'Sandy', McCorkle was known as a 'scrappy' type, and the man largely responsi-

ble for putting 'real fight' into the 31st, which duly gave its pilots the confidence that led to them scoring a string of victories for the Group, and the Fifteenth in general.

The honour of becoming the first Mustang aces in the MTO went to young ex-'Eagle' Squadron pilot Frederick Trafton. Joining the 308th FG during its Spitfire Mk VIII period, he was awarded a 'damaged' Bf 109. Things improved for Trafton with the advent of the P-51, and on 18 April he destroyed a Bf 109 over Udine during an aerodrome attack by the 31st.

The 21 April mission to Ploesti, when only the B-17 elements of the bomber force heard the bad weather recall signal, found the 31st covering B-24s just as they made their bombing runs. Heavily engaged with about 30 Bf 109s which then attacked the Liberators, Trafton shot down one at 35,000 ft, and claimed a second as a probable.

Victories three, four and five fell to Trafton on 23 April. The bombers' target was the Messerschmitt works at Weiner Neustadt and the 308th FS had been assigned to a force of 107 B-24s which, unknown to the fighter pilots, had delayed their take-off by one hour. Fred Trafton's 'Yellow' Flight met with the 'big friends' just before the Initial Point on their bomb run over Lake Balatine, in Hungary. Trafton then found his second element lagging behind, and a call established the cause as oxygen failure. He and his wingman, 2nd Lt George Hughes, dropped back to cover their colleagues and soon spotted three Bf 109s.

Half-rolling, Trafton tried drawing the German fighters into combat, and as he did so, three Macchi C.202s passed across his sights in line astern. It was too good a chance to miss and the Mustang pilot opened fire, scoring hits on all three Italian fighters. Two of them crashed before 'Yellow' Flight wheeled back to protect the second element of P-51s, which had been temporarily taken in hand by a besieged George Hughes.

In the MTO, the First Tactical Air Force – a temporary formation composed of Ninth and Twelfth AAF units, plus other Allied air force squadrons – included the 111th TRS, which divided its aircraft complement into flights and identified each machine by a single letter, followed by a second aircraft ID letter. In 1945, these F-6Cs belonged to 'C' Flight, the second aircraft in line coded 'CQ' bearing the name *Darling Meg* or *May* (*USAF*)

However, while Trafton had been in combat, Hughes had been forced to bail out of his crippled Mustang after HE shells had punctured his engine cowling. Trafton circled but could not spot the chute canopy of his wingman.

Noting more enemy fighters climbing towards the P-51s, Trafton dived on them, despite now being low on ammunition. Three Bf 109s attacked him and a cannon shell shattered his canopy and instruments, putting 95 assorted fragments into his body. Trafton managed to bail out at 700 ft, and on reaching the ground was greeted by a band of partisans. He succeeded in reaching Allied lines and subsequent analysis of his combat record showed that his aerial victories had all gone down between 1300 and 1345, beating the victories scored by Charles McCorkle by about 15 minutes. McCorkle's three kills on this mission made him the second Mustang ace in the theatre, although he had already achieved that status in Spitfires.

FRANTIC TO RUSSIA

On 2 June 1944 the Fifteenth mounted the first of its *Frantic* shuttle-bombing missions to Russia when 130 B-17s, escorted by the 'Checker-tails' P-51s, flew to Poltava via their en route target, the Debrecen marshalling yards in Hungary. Lt Col Chester Sluder led the Mustangs, and selected fighter groundcrews rode in 2nd BG B-17s, which were part of the five-group bomber force that pressed on to land at the Ukranian airfields of Poltava and Mirgorod, while 64 of the 325th's fighters put down at Piryatin. On 6 June, a day understandably overshadowed by events at Normandy, 104 Fifteenth AAF B-17s sortied from the USSR to place their bombs on Galati, in Rumania. Reaction by the Luftwaffe resulted in Roy Hogg, CO of the 318th FS, becoming an ace, his two Fw 190 victories being his fifth and sixth kills. Robert Barkey got his fifth, a Bf 109, while Wayne Lowry also opened his score – he would finish with 11 kills all told. A Ju 88 was also shot down by Lt Cullen J Hoffman of the 317th to make his fifth, and thus give the 'Clan' three aces on this top secret mission.

The 52nd FG took the bombers to Munich on 9 June, the escort claiming a total score of 14 for no losses – a feat which resulted in the award of the group's first Distinguished Unit Citation; two days later the shuttle bombers returned home to Italy, this time dropping their loads on another Rumanian target, the airfield at Foscani, en route.

On 15 June the dangers inherent in strafing were brought home to the 52nd when, on a tactical mission to support *Anvil* (the invasion of Southern France), the Group lost no less than seven P-51s. The following day the Mustang pilots were more than relieved to be back on bomber escort, which was, at that stage of the war in the aircraft they were flying, a far safer option!

The 52nd did well that day, meeting the Hungarian 101st 'Puma' Group and shooting down ten of their Bf 109Gs. P-51s of the 2nd FS engaged 55 German fighters over Czechoslovakia, and 'Sully' Varnell scored his third double kill on a single mission. During this combat he managed to dissuade a German pilot from attacking a crippled bomber, despite the fact that his P-51B's guns had jammed.

Ploesti was 'on the board' again on 23 June, which turned out to be the 52nd's best day of the war. Up against the redoubtable JG 52, which was having a tough job defending the now-battered oil-fields, Group pilots claimed 12 Bf

Like all other groups in the MTO, the 52nd FG also adopted bright tail markings as 1944 progressed, yellow being the colour chosen in their case – these are clearly visible in this shot, despite the photographer's rather unfortunate cropping of 'WD-M' in the foreground. As with the 31st FG, the 52nd had earlier flown Spitfires within the Fifteenth AAF from late 1943. Transition from one Merlin-engined aircraft to another was therefore relatively trouble-free, although being able to traverse the Alps and fly into all of Eastern Europe was a revelation to pilots more used to the very short-ranged Supermarine fighter (*USAF*)

109Gs to bring the 52nd's combined total to 102 victories in 30 days – a theatre record that was never beaten. The dogfights of the 23rd were also to see Bf 109s fall to 'Herky' Green of the 325th for his 15th kill, and one to John Voll to open his tally, although three P-51s were lost. Four were actually claimed, all of them by Erich Hartmann of I./JG 52.

With 'Sully' Varnell tying with Green for top slot in the Fifteenth's fighter ace table, there was a healthy rivalry between the two men. Green, however, went one better by also destroying his 16th aircraft on this particular Ploesti mission.

It was the oilfields yet again for the 325th on 24 June, the American pilots shooting down five enemy aircraft. They included two Rumanian I.A.R.81Cs, a number of which were to be lost defending local targets, although they were not always recognised as such in US pilots' after-action reports. Thomas Lowry's fifth and sixth kills were scored on this mission, although one P-51 was lost in return.

The 31st continued its fine record against the Luftwaffe on 26 June when Maj Sam Brown and his wingman tackled another 50 enemy fighters during a bomber escort mission. This time Brown destroyed four and damaged two, but most importantly, broke up the *Jagdfliegers'* carefully orchestrated attack on the bombers. Like most American fighter pilots, Brown knew full well that once the Germans were forced to scatter they did not have time to reform into large groups where their mass firepower could be devastating. Once split up, they not only became easier meat for the escorts to pick off, but in ones or twos were far less of a threat to individual bomber boxes.

Heavily engaged by the enemy on 28 June, the 325th had escorted the bombers to Bucharest when 50 or so fighters attacked them. In the ensuing melée the 'Checkertails' showed their mettle by destroying 17 of the enemy's fighters without sustaining any losses themselves.

P-51D *MISS CATHIE* of the 317th FS, flown by Lt David E Ambrose, who scored his second kill in this aircraft on 19 January 1945. Having cut their teeth on P-47s, the 'Checkertail Clan' showed they had conceded nothing to the old Spitfire groups by flying a shuttle mission to Russia a week after the first P-51s arrived (*Crow*)

On 6 July 'Sully' Varnell reached the zenith of his combat career with a triple score over the Ploesti area, bringing him a total of 17 victories, two Silver Stars and two DFCs. Rotated home to train new pilots, Varnell was tragically killed in a flying accident in Florida the following spring.

Despite the P-51 groups meeting substantial numbers of enemy fighters on some missions, they were more than able to cope and continued to accrue victories. Frustratingly, low cloud and rain conspired to keep the entire Fifteenth Air Force on the ground for days on end during autumn. Accordingly, the Luftwaffe and RSI failed to suffer an attrition rate quite as high as that of the *Jagdwaffe* in western Europe, and with fighter output in Germany steadily rising as a result of an emergency programme, a substantial number of interceptor fighters remained available. Also, by this late stage of the war the question for defenders was often whether they would accept the risk inherent in taking on the sleek silver Mustangs 'riding shotgun' for the Liberators and Fortresses. On occasion, common sense prevailed over valour.

Tactics conferences regularly brought the group leaders together to discuss the latest war situation, enemy strength and myriad other things that made for an efficient organisation able to maintain hard-won air superiority. In this view P-51Ds flown by commanders of three of the Fifteenth's four Mustang groups – front to rear, the 31st, 52nd and 332nd FGs – have been parked while their owners attend the meeting (*USAF*)

Not that the Luftwaffe had totally used up all its experienced fighter pilots. Although such individuals were now in the minority, they continued to give even the P-51 a good run for its money. On the other hand, German pilots coming upon the 31st FG could not know that it was advisable to avoid the aircraft being flown by Capt Norman Skogstad! Known as the best shot in the 31st, Skogstad commanded the 307th FS, and had previously been a gunnery instructor. Other pilots were in awe at 'Norm's' ability behind the P-51's reflector sight, and it was said that 'Jerry wasn't safe even in a 89° deflection break'!

As was common knowledge at the time, it took opportunity, skill and luck, combined in good measure, to turn a pilot into an ace. The latter quality was something that defied definition, although individuals took steps to shorten the odds a little. On 19 May 1943 'Herky' Green had been badly shot up when flying a P-40F numbered 13, and he never tempted fate again – Green eventually became the 325th's top ace with 18 kills (5 in P-51s), and always made a point of flying aircraft number 11.

On 22 July 1944 the Fifteenth laid on a bold mission – an all-fighter shuttle to Russia. The 31st drew the escort task and provided 58 P-51s to cover 76 P-38s of the 82nd FG, plus some F-5s from the 5th Photo Recon Group. Codenamed *Frantic III*, this and other shuttle missions to Russia were devised tens of thousands of miles away in the Pentagon, far from the muddy fighter fields of Italy. And this one had an added wrinkle. Intelligence reports had been received about a Luftwaffe base in southwestern Poland which purportedly held a number of slightly damaged American fighters repainted in German markings. These aircraft had been observed shadowing heavy bombers, and the upshot was that the base, Mielec,

Tempus Fugit makes a neat portrait on a typical Italian airfield in 1944. The mount of Col William A Daniel, five-victory ace of the 308th FS, this P-51D bears the red diagonal Group recognition stripes on the tail, an outgrowth of the original single diagonal red stripe that identified the 31st FG for a short time (*via E A Munday*)

was to be attacked and all facilities and aircraft found on it destroyed.

So important was this mission deemed to be that Brig Gen Dean 'Doc' Strother, CO of the 306th FW, flew a P-51 as part of the main formation when it duly took off and headed for Poltava, in the Ukraine, on the 22nd. At Poltava, Gen Strother briefed Maj Gen Permonoff, area commander of the Russian forces, and Maj Gen Bob Walsh, US Attaché in Moscow. The primary target was to be attacked on the 25th, and despite Soviet objections (which had been anticipated), the Americans had orders to fly the mission no matter what their Allies tried to do to delay it.

At the mission brief, details were uncharacteristically well noted by the pilots, who realised the risk of getting lost over the vast hinterland of Russia – Mielec is situated some 600 miles west of Poltava. Among the attention-grabbing facts for this sortie were that Russian maps were inaccurate, local radar not very dependable, there was no estimate of enemy aircraft in the target area and the ground battle lines were fluid. The American pilots were also told to avoid all Russian aircraft, and in the event that they were attacked they were to engage their 'allies' swiftly and effectively

Take-off and rendezvous were accomplished smoothly, and with the P-51s acting as top cover, the Lightnings went in at low-level. The P-38s actually missed the juiciest target, however, for Mielec was at that time a temporary base for the *Stukageschwader* led by the legendary Hans Ulrich Rudel.

Shortly before the American force appeared, all three *Staffeln* of a single *Gruppe* of Ju 87s had taken off. As the airfield appeared deserted, Maj Sam Brown, 307th FS CO, ordered a sweeping left turn, and there directly below was a German motorised column. Sixteen P-51s raked the convoy, leaving many vehicles burning and a large number of Wehrmacht troops dead. The toll included a Ju 52 that lumbered across Lt Jim Brooks' sights and was promptly shot down.

Lt Jim Brooks of the 307th FS in typical 'sunny Italy' pose on the wing of his personal P-51D (rather unusually named *February*), which exhibits part of his 13-kill score. Brooks was the second-top scorer in the squadron, two victories behind Sam Brown. Unfortunately for AAF planners, Italy was often a complete let-down as far as good flying weather was concerned, a fact that tended to reduce the bombing effort, and thereby lengthen the war in what was always a difficult theatre (*R Goebel*)

He was amongst those pilots now worried at the remaining fuel in the Mustangs' tanks, but 15 minutes off target en route to Poltava the Americans spotted something no fighter pilot could pass up. Into view came Rudel's Stukas, bombing and strafing the Russians in the vicinity of Jaroslav. Without hesitation eight P-51s climbed to counter any high cover mounted by the *Jagdwaffe* while the other eight, including ace Maj Ernest Shipman, fell on the Ju 87s and destroyed 27 of them before their critical fuel state forced them to break off. Rudel's own *Staffel* escaped the slaughter, but the Americans were elated. And so too were their Russian hosts, vodka flowing freely as confirmation of the kills came in.

The 307th's Mustangs had strafed Rumanian targets before reaching Russia on their outboard leg of the mission, and by the time the unit had returned home to San Severo on the 26th, the score had risen to over 40 aircraft destroyed, plus vehicles wrecked and German personnel killed – small wonder that *Frantic III* resulted in the 31st FG's second DUC. On the debit side the cost of the mission was heavy, with 10 P-51s and 20 P-38s being lost, nine of the latter claimed by Bf 109Gs of the Rumanian 9th Fighter Regiment, without loss to themselves.

Medals were awarded for outstanding acts of air leadership and courage in all war theatres, and the MTO was no exception. The Silver Star, the fourth-highest US decoration, was presented to a number of fighter pilots, and one proud recipient for his action on 25 July was Capt Barry

Wearing the distinctive red stripes of the 31st FG, a four-ship from the 308th FS is put through its paces for the USAAF cameraman early in 1944. The 31st, like other MTO P-51 Groups, flew mainly -5 models without the fin fillet. 'HL-C', alias *OKaye,* was the mount of 10.5 kill ace Capt Leland Molland, who scored his first four victories in the Spitfire Mk VIII, whilst the aircraft nearest to the camera (44-13504) is being flown here by 5-kill ace Capt Jack Smith. Ironically, this P-51D was nicknamed '*OK*', and was later shot down having been re-coded 'HL-L' and renamed *Smokey* (*USAF via H Holmes*)

Lawler (11 kills) of the 52nd FG. During a bomber escort to Austria, Lawler assumed command of the Group when the regular lead was forced to abort. Leading his P-51s into some 40 enemy fighters bent on attacking the bombers, Lawler was gratified to see them break to counter the Mustangs, with the result that none managed to reach the bombers – he accounted for two fighters in the ensuing action.

Rounding out July was another Ploesti mission on the 28th. This time the 31st's Leland Molland made the headlines by scoring the 306th FW's 1000th victory, but the month had been a sobering one for the Fifteenth AAF, as it had lost a staggering 318 bombers in action – this figure was the highest ever experienced by the Fifteenth in World War 2.

One of the more unfortunate 'kills' claimed during this period was due to an error in aircraft recognition that occurred on 30 July. Maj Ernest Shipman was the victim when his P-51 was shot down near Budapest by a P-38. With seven victories to his credit at that time, Shipman was obliged to spend the rest of the war as a PoW.

Fighter pilot losses for most of July had been lighter than those experienced by the bomber groups, but the downing of experienced men was always sorely felt, and on 31 July the 52nd FG lost not only two pilots – one a near ace – but also their respective P-51Bs to another mistake. Lt Edmund Gubler and Lt Dennis Riddle, who formed an element of the 2nd FS, were dogfighting Bf 109s in cumulus cloud near Ploesti that day. When the German fighters appeared, Gubler and Riddle became separated from the rest of their squadron. The latter, who had four victories to his credit, spotted a Bf 109 and chased it in and out of cloud, thus losing sight of Gubler. As Riddle suddenly emerged from cloud, his wingman fired almost on reflex, mistaking his friend for the German.

With his engine on fire, Riddle had little choice but to jump from very low altitude, his chute barely having time to deploy before he was on the ground. Despite this he landed unharmed and was startled to see Gubler's aircraft put down in a nearby field, intent on picking him up. With the shorter Gubler perched on Riddle's lap, the Merlin was gunned for take-off. But rather than taxy, the Mustang gradually dug itself into the soft earth, to the point where the propeller touched and the P-51 somersaulted onto its back. Fighting their way out of their Plexiglas cage, both pilots were captured by the Germans and in early October 1944 were liberated by the Red Army from a prison camp in Bucharest.

Higher authority tended to look benevolently on such actions until pick ups went wrong. Losing two pilots and two aircraft instead of one of each was unacceptable, and a ban was posted. It was not always complied with, however, much to the lasting relief of those men who came back by this unconventional means.

After another crack at Ploesti on 10 August there was a slight change of emphasis for both fighter and bomber groups, with the invasion of southern France commencing on the 15th. Escorted by Italian-based P-51 and P-38 groups, the 'heavies' softened up the invasion area between the 12th and 16th. With troops ashore it was then back to 'business as usual', which for the Fifteenth's bombers meant further pounding of Ploesti.

But relief from attacking a target that was invariably well defended by fighters and flak was at hand. Rumania lay directly in the path of the advancing Red Army and after two more AAF bombing raids, on 17 and 19 August, those particular oil refineries came off the target list for good. On the former mission the Rumanians suffered heavily with nine aircraft destroyed by the 31st FG. Among the casualties was Capt Alexandre Serbanescu, who had 50 victories to his credit. Ploesti was captured by the Russians on 30 August.

To hasten the end of the Third Reich the Fifteenth AAF offered material support to the Russians by keeping the Luftwaffe effectively out of the picture, and on 31 August 48 P-51s of the 52nd FG went on a strafing spree to Reghin aerodrome in Rumania, claiming nine air victories for three P-51s lost. In addition, for a mission which won the 52nd its second DUC, the fighters claimed 60 enemy aircraft destroyed on the ground.

September saw the P-51 pilots briefed to attack more ground targets, with sorties ranging into Yugoslavia to hit Ecke and Ilandza, as well as sweeps flown over Greece, where on the 15th the 325th shot down two Ju 52s. Only ten more aircraft were to fall to Mustangs for the entire month.

An unusual incident occurred on 29 August when the 4th FS escorted B-17s and B-24s to Czechoslovakia. Dropping down to carry out customary strafing attacks on anything of interest, the pilots found an airfield harbouring roughly 100 Me 323 transports, which the Americans proceeded to systematically shoot up until their ammunition was exhausted. Two days later there came an unexpected opportunity to finish the job.

Forward fuselage close-up of Leland Molland's *OKaye*, with his kills taking the form of a neat line of black crosses below the cockpit. If anything, the personal markings of MTO-based Mustang groups were a little more restrained than was the case elsewhere in the USAAF (*via Mackay*)

Maj James Tyler, the 4th FS commander, led a flight of four P-51s to the same area, and he duly strafed the remaining intact Me 323s, the rest having meanwhile been bulldozed into a large heap. Tyler's flight then crossed the border into Hungary to shoot up an unprotected marshalling yard. Their ammo low, the P-51s prepared to return home when Lt Fred Straut spotted a train on the move. Receiving permission to make one strafing pass, Straut led his wingman, Lt Charles Wilson, down on the train.

The tried and tested technique for 'busting' trains was to disable the locomotive by bursting its boiler and then hit every tenth car. Invariably this wrecked the entire train, and more often than not set it ablaze. Wilson noted that as he was about to shoot up the tenth car, the locomotive gave off a huge cloud of steam as the driver frantically opened the valves to give the impression that his boiler had already blown. Wilson was not fooled, however. He dropped down to 75 ft and poured 200 rounds of API into the locomotive's cab.

This time the boiler did blow – a bit too spectacularly for the hurtling Mustang. Pieces as lethal as shrapnel flew through the air to puncture the cooling system of Wilson's aircraft

and burn off the fabric covering of the ailerons and tail surfaces. Clawing for altitude, his P-51 reached 5000 ft, where it was looked over by Straut. It was not good. The seized engine was by now alight, and as flames streamed over the canopy Wilson decided to 'hit the silk'.

He made ready, cut the radio and engine switches and was about to vacate the cockpit when the fire went out. Wilson climbed back in, radioed Straut and opted to belly the aircraft into a large field ahead. Safely down, and having avoided cracking his head on the gunsight, Wilson waited. Just before he had cut his radio switch, Maj Wyatt Exum, the fourth pilot in the flight had called, 'I'll be down to get you, Charlie'.

As good as his word Exum, who was on his first mission with the 52nd after a tour in the Pacific, made a perfect landing. However, his aircraft's tailwheel stuck fast in a drainage ditch at the end of his roll out and he couldn't make the necessary turn into wind for take-off. Putting his back under the tail, Wilson lifted the rear end clear. Exum gunned the engine and Wilson scrambled aboard with bullets from mounted German troops, who had swiftly rushed to the scene, whistling about their ears. Tyler had strafed these newcomers but had not completely deterred them. Parachutes discarded to make room, the two men arranged themselves as best they could, Wilson crouching behind and above Exum as he handled the take-off. The former literally rode shotgun, blazing away at the riders with his .45. Unimpressed with his passenger's marksmanship, however, Exum was glad when his colleague threw the pistol away!

Climbing out to 12,000 ft with Maj Tyler on the wing, the two-pilot Mustang proceeded to climb to 25,000 in order to come within range of 'Big Fence', the radar homing station near Ancona. Exum received a vector to home base, although by the time the overloaded Mustang approached the Adriatic, the fuel state was marginal. Rather than risk a landing in Yugoslavia, the pilots made a bid for home base, making it back with little more than fumes left in the fuel tanks to turn the Merlin over. Maj Exum subsequently received the Silver Star for his rescue of Wilson.

Commanding the 5th FS of the 52nd FG since June 1944 had been Col Ralph J 'Doc' Watson. Having flown a tour on P-38s, he had taken well to the P-51, and on 12 October was leading the group on a low-level aerodrome attack on Seregeyles, in Hungary, some 400 miles from home base. The entire flight was made at tree-top height in less than ideal weather conditions, and upon reaching the target area Watson realised the P-51s had achieved total surprise.

No doubt stealing some Colonel or Group Captain's thunder, a humble naval Lieutenant gingerly touches down in southern France, and thus becomes the first Allied aviator to land in the region since 1940, following the launch of *Dragoon* – the invasion of the former Vichy held territory in mid-1944. The pilot of the 111th TRS Mustang, nicknamed *Val Gal II*, was forced down by a loose canopy

The yellow-tailed Mustangs proceeded to thoroughly work over the field, shooting down five aircraft that were unfortunate enough to be airborne as the American fighters roared over. All P-51s reached home safely, although some were damaged by enemy fire, Watson's among them. He counted at least 12 holes in the airframe and a 40 mm shell, collected during a barge strafe, had not improved the cockpit design!

Attempting at the eleventh hour to obtain at least local air superiority through quality if not quantity, the Luftwaffe had a potentially deadly fighter in the turbojet Messerschmitt Me 262. That its performance was superior to all Allied piston-engined fighters was soon manifestly clear through numerous sightings and reports, but until 22 December none had fallen to a Fifteenth AAF fighter.

That changed when the two 31st FG pilots, Lts Eugene McGlauflin and Roy Scales, nailed an Me 262 while escorting a PR aircraft over Germany. This latter duty was not exactly welcomed by the pilots, but the previously immune Mosquitos now faced a serious challenge from the Me 262, which had to be countered with the best conventional fighters then available.

That the Me 262 was the 'wave of the future' was in little doubt. Good as the P-51 and other piston-engined fighters were, turbojet powerplants and swept wings had already rendered conventional combat aircraft obsolete. Not that this prevented Allied pilots from giving the German jets a run for their money, but numerous encounters ended in frustration when the enemy used its superior performance to break off combat.

P-51s were heavily involved with Me 262s on occasions, but the experience of the 370th FG, which converted from P-38s during January-February 1945, was typical of the outcome of many skirmishes involving Mustangs and jets. Pilots such as Marion Owens, Glen Caldwell and Ian Mackenzie fired at Me 262s and all duly received 'damaged' credits, while Richard Stevenson managed a half claim for the destruction of an Me 262, but no 370th FG pilot had a confirmed jet victory to himself. These, and other P-51 flyers, would be the first to admit that more doubt remained over a jet 'probable' or 'damaged' claim than with conventional fighters.

Fortunately for the Allies, the German aero industry had long been hamstrung by poor materials, disrupted manufacture and severely curtailed pilot conversion training, all of which meant that the jet fighter programme, which had held such promise, was fatally compromised. By thrusting the Me 262 into the frontline before it had been fully tested (particularly in the area of engine reliability), the Luftwaffe lost any advantage it might have otherwise achieved – but by late 1944 it had little choice.

January 1945 brought some of the worst weather ever to hit the continent of Europe, and a consequent drastic curtailment of Allied air operations all along the front. If anything, the conditions affected the Fifteenth AAF 'heavies' more than their colleagues in the Eighth and Ninth Air Forces, and many winter days saw no air activity whatsoever. Fighter operations were similarly reduced, the 325th flying on just 11 days during the month, with three of these dates representing six sorties or less by the P-51s. With the Luftwaffe conspicuous by its absence, the 'Checker-

This view of 11-kill ace Lt Bob Goebel makes for a classic shot for the war correspondents as he sits perched on the cockpit sill of his 31st FG P-51D *Flying Dutchman*. The score speaks for itself, although the MTO was a war theatre where the publicity usually afforded such prowess at the controls of a fighter was not quite so lavish as was the case elsewhere. War correspondents – and USO shows – were thinner on the ground in Italy, and relatively little publicity was afforded the fighting units of the Fifteenth AAF (*R Goebel*)

tails' turned their guns on other targets, including trains, and sweeps into Yugoslavia notched up dozens of locomotives left with burst boilers, useless to the Germans.

March saw little appreciable increase in aerial opposition to Allied air dominance as the Third Reich was forced to systematically cede territory, crushed between massive armies advancing from east and west. Under a general directive to place Fifteenth AAF fighters nearer to the remaining action, the 31st moved to Mondolfo on the 3rd.

On the 22nd Capt William Dillard (6 kills) of the 31st FG shot down an Me 262, the first to fall to a Fifteenth Air Force pilot since the previous December. An estimated 25 to 30 Me 262s were encountered over Ruhland, and five of them were claimed as damaged. Col William Daniel (5 kills), then CO of the 31st, shot down another Me 262 two days later over Berlin when the Group's Mustangs came home with a score of five jet fighters destroyed. Three jets had also fallen to pilots of the all-Negro 332nd FG – namely Lts Roscoe Brown, Robert W Williams and Samuel Watts.

The four squadrons within this Group had already forged an enviable reputation not only for their combat ability, but also for conscientiously escorting bombers, and on 24 March the 'heavies' were well covered when the Fifteenth AAF mounted its longest mission of the war. From their Italian bases, Berlin was a 1600-mile round trip for the bomber crews, who were mighty glad to see the red-tailed Mustangs 'locked' in place to deter the Luftwaffe for the entire duration of the mission.

On 25 March the Fifteenth Air Force heavy bombers attacked targets in the Czech capital Prague, and when the last bomber turned for home, the strategic war on the southern front from bases in Italy was at an end. There was now little left to bomb.

Fighter sorties continued, however. On 31 March the box score was 35 aerial victories, the 31st's 20 giving it 'top dog' position, as well as the highest tally in the MTO with a total of 567 kills. The 332nd meanwhile claimed 13 to record its most productive day. Three enemy aircraft fell to the 325th on 2 April, the same day that the record number of Fifteenth FC sorties flown in a 24-hour period was set at 409.

The 'Checkertails' again made their mark on 11 April with a victory over the Luftwaffe's remarkable Arado Ar 234 *Blitz* bomber, while the Group also claimed the 12th and last of the Fifteenth AAF's Me 262 victories on the 18th. German jet bomber sorties on 11 April also netted an Ar 234 for the 52nd FG, which claimed it as the first example to go down over northern Italy – the Luftwaffe had based a number of Ar 234s in that area, primarily for high-speed reconnaissance flights.

A tremendous tactical bombing effort was mounted by Fifteenth AAF 'heavies' on 15 April when no less than 1235 B-24s and B-17s, escorted

An anonymous F-6C of the 111th TRS provides the backdrop for this album snapshot. The steely-eyed fellow in the foreground is Bronze Star winner SSgt Cooper, although just what his connection is with this aircraft remains a mystery. Aside from wearing an impressive tally of successfully completed photo-recon (stencilled cameras) and artillery spotting (stencilled binoculars) sorties on its nose, this Mustang, also boasts a kill marking beneath the cockpit (*Anderson via Ivie*)

As the war drew to its inevitable conclusion, groundcrews of the 'Checkertail Clan' had time to extend their Group's black and yellow marking to P-51 undercarriage doors and the forward portion of drop tanks, and many aircraft had their previously abbreviated tail markings extended forward and neatly edged off. This particular machine, *Three Bees*, was flown by Maj John R Burman, the final CO of the 317th FS

by 586 fighters, ranged across the remaining territory held by the Germans. In common with virtually all Allied fighter formations in Europe, the war for the Fifteenth's Mustang units was ending not in a series of 'last ditch' air battles, but a relentless hunting down of an elusive, but still-aggressive, quarry and a gruelling series of ground attack sorties against myriad targets that remained dangerous when still defended by flak batteries.

On, or about, 24 April the 52nd made its second base move of its Mustang period by occupying Piagiolino, and the following day the Group joined the 'Checkertails' for a ground-strafing mission. That day was also the last time that Fifteenth AAF four-engined bombers were called upon to operate in combat.

When, finally, on 8 May the Germans capitulated, Allied fighter squadrons equipped with short-range types were flying from a number of airfields in Reich territory – absolute proof, if further was needed, of how total the defeat was. Having fighter-bombers based a few minutes' flying time from the frontlines had greatly assisted ground commanders in the final phases of the war, while Mustangs, almost irrespective of where they had been based, had provided a long-range shield that proved all but impenetrable to the enemy. Few combat aircraft have ever had as much of an effect on the outcome of a single conflict as North American's superlative fighter.

Among the statistics generated by the long, hard, war in southern Europe was the fact on 87,732 fighter sorties, a score of 1496 enemy aircraft had been destroyed in aerial combat. This figure had to be set against the loss of 156 AAF fighters in the air, and a further 232 to ground fire – a highly respectable achievement by the 'country cousins', as the southern-based groups were sometimes disparagingly referred to by their colleagues in the 'cushier' ETO.

The P-51s of the Fifteenth Air Force had also set something of a record by escorting American bombers to targets in no less than 11 countries – Italy, France, Germany, Poland, Czechoslovakia, Austria, Hungary, Bulgaria, Rumania, Yugoslavia, and Greece. In addition, they had also flown over Russia, whilst certain seasoned individuals who had flown tours with MTO-based groups in the pre-P-51 period were able to better even this impressive total by adding England and several Middle Eastern countries to their geographical tallies as well!

The Allied ascendancy over the Axis powers was so much due to the advent of the P-51 that its importance to the cause would be hard to overestimate. In monetary terms too, the North American fighter represented excellent value. In 1944 it had been, at $51,572 a copy, the third-cheapest fighter the AAF procured after the Curtiss P-40 and Bell P-39, but by the following year the price had dropped to $50,985. And as production of both the Warhawk and Airacobra had, by this stage of the war, been completed, the Mustang was now the cheapest combat aircraft in any category that the Army purchased.

THE FIGHTING 'RED TAILS'

Of the four Mustang-equipped fighter groups of the Fifteenth Air Force, only one did not officially produce an ace. This same outfit scored fewer victories over enemy aircraft than the other three, and was damned in an official report. This was the 332nd FG, the only Negro-manned unit in the US Army Air Force. The bald and highly selective 'facts' outlined above are still the common view of the unit. And yet, in many respects, it would not be unfair to describe the 332nd as the most successful Mustang fighter group in the MTO.

Prevailing attitudes were hostile to the very idea of using Negro pilots, and a secret 1925 war college report had damned the entire Negro race as mentally inferior, immoral and 'rank cowards in the dark'. When black pilots were accepted for training, it was as a result of political expediency, and many senior army officers were bigots who expected and even wanted the so-called Tuskegee experiment to fail. They looked for failure, and consistently denied the 332nd FG the opportunity to shine.

Because the Army Air Corps had had no Negro pilots before 1942, and because they could not be allowed to fly with white fighter units, the Negro squadrons could have no nucleus of experienced pilots around which to form. The Group was the last in the Fifteenth Air Force to receive Mustangs, and was assigned fewer missions than its rivals, thus encountering fewer enemy aircraft. Many claims by Negro pilots were disallowed or downgraded, and the evidence seems to show that high-scoring pilots from the unit were quickly sent home before they could become aces, with the attendant (unwelcome) publicity.

Remarkably, many very high calibre Negroes flocked to the colours, determined to do their patriotic duty, even for a country which hated them. One of the joint top-scoring Tuskegee pilots, Lee Archer, later remembered that 'I did feel it was ironic that we were fighting a fascist country for one that was, in our estimation, almost as bad. You wondered whether it was worthwhile, but I thought that Hitler and Germany were the greater risk to us as black people than the racism in America. It was a more virulent type and I was very set

A young 2nd Lt Luke Weathers (far right) discusses with fellow trainee pilots the route for their next flight. This posed shot was taken at Tuskegee Army Airfield in late 1942 as the all-black 332nd FG was involved in an intensive work up on war-weary P-40s prior to their assignment to the MTO a year later

Much criticism was levelled at the performance of the 332nd by bigoted senior officers both in-theatre and in the Pentagon, but a close study of the operational statistics reveals that the Group matched or exceeded other fighter outfits in the Fifteenth in terms of mission effectiveness. Only in the area of aircraft maintenance was the 'Red Tails'' proficiency lower, and that was primarily due to the rawness of their all-Negro groundcrew, who had trained on less sophisticated fighter types like the P-39 and P-40. Nevertheless, despite their initially poor readiness rates, the 332nd worked at the problem and eventually achieved a figure of 85 per cent by war's end, just 3.6 per cent lower than the all-white groups in-theatre

on doing everything I could to stop it. I always thought when this is over they'll change'.

Other pilots felt similar emotions. 'Each mission I flew, each bomb I dropped and every bullet I fired against the Nazis was also directed against racism and white supremacy in America', recalled Luke Weathers, one of Archer's squadron mates.

But it is not the case that there needs to be a more generous reading of the history of the Tuskegee airmen – their record speaks for itself and needs neither explanation nor apology. If the Fifteenth Air Force Mustang units are compared only over the period during which the 332nd FG was equipped with the P-51, the unit's record stands up to the closest scrutiny. Between August 1944 and April 1945, for example, the 332nd accounted for well over a quarter of the total kills by the four groups in fewer missions and fewer encounters with enemy aircraft.

The only area in which there was a noticeable discrepancy between the 332nd and the other groups operating in the Mediterranean was maintenance. Strict segregation made it impossible to use a core of experienced (white) engineers so, like the pilots, the groundcrew were almost all newly graduated from training, and only beginning to build up the experience which could be taken for granted in the rest of the air force. Very few black Americans had any prior mechanical training or experience before they joined the Air Corps, but morale and motivation were high. Statistics would seem to indicate that the 332nd maintained a readiness rate of 85 per cent, which compares with 88.6 per cent for the white groups.

Even had the Group's record of downing enemy fighters been less impressive, the unit could still lay claim to being the most efficient Mustang outfit. A public preoccupation with aces and fighter-versus-fighter combat has distracted attention from the fact that the primary role of the P-51 was to protect USAAF bombers, and to ensure that these reached their targets and returned to base safely. And, uniquely among the USAAF's fighter groups, the 332nd could claim never to have lost a bomber in its charge.

This was a fantastic achievement, due in no small part to the iron discipline imposed by the charismatic group commander, Benjamin Davis, who drilled it into his pilots that their job was to protect the bombers, and not to go chasing off after Messerschmitts and glory. 'Too often the fighters left the bombers to go chasing enemy fighters and personal glory. Davis said that "Your job is to keep enemy fighters away from the bombers. Your job is not to shoot down enemy fighters and become an ace"', remembered Woodrow Crockett, a long-serving pilot with the unit. Such was the awe in which Ben Davis was held, many of his high-spirited young pilots would not have dreamed of disobeying his dictat! 'I never considered wandering off', recalled Lee Archer, 'and I'm a pretty independent person! '

Initially, a single black fighter squadron, the 99th, had formed as an experiment, and had been sent to North Africa where it flew P-40s in the ground attack and dive-bomber roles. The unit commenced operations in June 1943, later transferring to the 79th FG. The squadron's CO, Lt Col Benjamin O Davis, was recalled to take command of the 332nd FG in October 1943.

The 332nd had activated at Tuskegee Army Airfield on 13 October 1942, with the 100th, 301st and 302nd FSs as its component units. These squadrons had undergone training on decidedly war-weary P-40s, but the Group arrived in Italy with P-39s on 3 February 1944 before transitioning onto P-47s that April.

Combat operations began on 7 June, with a 32-aircraft fighter sweep of the Ferrara-Bologna area.

The Group scored its first kills during its third mission, a bomber escort flight to Munich. The P-47 marked a welcome improvement over the P-39 and P-40, but was to be short-lived in 332nd FG service, P-51Bs and Cs arriving from late June. The pioneer 99th FS finally joined the 332nd FG at its new base at Ramitelli, on the Adriatic coast, on 28 June 1944. The move was not universally popular with the combat-hardened veterans of the 99th, who regarded the 332nd as raw newcomers, and who saw their removal from the white 79th FG as being a return to segregation.

The P-47 flew its last mission on 30 June, while P-51 sorties began on 6 July. The Mustangs were secondhand, but the Group wasted no time in applying its colours – red tail units and spinners with nose bands in squadron colours.

The 332nd's first visit to Ploesti was undertaken on 13 July. Early offensives against the Rumanian oilfields had proved extraordinarily costly. The oil production area covered some 19 square miles, densely packed with refineries and pumping stations, but equally packed with anti-aircraft artillery and protected by the cream of German and Rumanian fighter units. There were even 2000 smoke generators, capable of shrouding the entire area with a thick artificial fog. Blast walls surrounded every installation, some as much as six feet thick and 20 feet high.

The Group escorted B-17s on a mission against railyards on 12 July 1944. Capt Joseph Elsberry led the flight, and shot down three Fw 190s on the mission, with a fourth enemy aircraft as a probable. Some 30 Fw 190s intercepted the bombers as they rendezvoused with their escort from the 332nd FG, who were circling at altitude. One moment the German pilots had a formation of unescorted B-17s in their sights, the next it was 'raining' Mustangs. Elsberry was the first black pilot to score three victo-

The most successful fighting outfits within the USAAF during World War 2 all had one thing in common – a strong, well-respected leader who flew with his pilots on virtually every mission. The 332nd were fortunate in having just such a man in Col Benjamin O Davis, who had already distinguished himself in combat over North Africa with the all-black 99th FS in 1943 before being given command of the fighting 'Red Tails'. He ruled with iron discipline, and drove home the message to his pilots that bomber protection was their one and only mission in life – a mission that the 332nd went on to perform better than any other group in the USAAF

Davis was well supported at unit level by four equally gifted squadron commanders, one of which, Capt Andrew 'Jug' Turner, is seen here ready to taxy out in his personal P-51C, *Skipper's Darlin' III*. His crew chief appears to be applying a tape covering over the gun ports, a quick job performed just prior to take-off which helped reduce the chances of moisture collecting in the the barrels of the .50 cals and turning to ice at altitude

P-51C *TOPPER III* of the 99th FS's Capt Ed Toppins. The four swastikas beneath the cockpit denote the quartet of kills claimed by the pilot in this aircraft during his tour with the 332nd (*USAF via Ivie*)

ries in the P-51, and the first to score three in a single mission.

On 16 July two Macchis were downed during a fighter sweep to Vienna, Lts Alfonso Davis and William Green intercepting the Italian fighters when they attempted to interfere with a straggling B-24 which the Tuskegee airmen were escorting home. Italy had already surrendered by this stage in the war, and the two Macchis belonged to the new Italian Socialist Republic air force in the north. German pilots encountered the following day fared little better. Three (of nineteen) enemy fighters attempted to attack bombers of the 306th BW, but were quickly shot down by Lts Robert and Luther Smith, and Lt Lawrence D Wilkens.

On 18 July 1944, Lt Clarence 'Lucky' Lester downed three Bf 109s to win himself a DFC. Lester's kills were among 11 scored by the Group that day, including two by Jack Holsclaw, one each by Walter Palmer, Ed Toppins, Charles Bailey, Hugh Warner, Roger Romine and a first for Lee Archer. This mission was the first to involve all four squadrons, and three of the Group's pilots were posted missing and a B-24 was lost to flak.

An escort mission to Friedrichshafen on 19 July netted four more enemy fighters for the 332nd, including a fourth confirmed kill for Joseph Elsberry, who became the Group's top scorer. Elsberry chased another enemy fighter to ground level, but failed to score the all-important fifth kill. Three B-24s fell to flak, but two stragglers were picked up near Udine, and these were escorted to safety. Lee Archer, who later overtook Elsberry, gained his second kill, chasing an enemy aircraft until it ran into a mountainside. Ed Toppins scored his third victory, while Langdon Johnson and Armour McDaniel opened their scores.

Things went badly on 25 July during an escort mission to the Herman Goring Tank Works at Linz. The Group lost two Mustangs, downing only one of the Bf 109s which attacked them. The Germans were experienced and lucky, concentrating on the weakest elements of the escort. Fortunately, the 332nd FG returned to form on 26 July, downing five Bf 109s. William Green, and Weldon Groves shared one kill, the others being credited to Freddie Hutchins, Leonard Jackson (his second victory) and Roger Romine. On 27 July, during a raid on the Weiss armament works at Budapest, four Bf 109s and four Fw 190s were downed, along with a single Reggiane Re.2001, by Edward Gleed and Alfred Gorham (two each), and by Claude Govan, Felix Kirkpatrick, Richard W Hall and Leonard Jackson.

Overall, July 1944 had been a busy month for the Group, resulting in 39 kills in nine missions between 12 and 30 July. German fighters tended to fly in formations which mimicked the USAAF escort fighters, staying at the bombers' level, and detaching small groups of fighters to lure away the real escorts. Col Davis' standing orders that his pilots were never to leave their charges prevented the 332nd from falling for this ruse.

August saw the Group escorting medium bombers softening up targets in preparation for the 15 August invasion of southern France, although it took time out to participate in three more escort missions to Ploesti. An escort mission to Budapest on 6 August resulted in a kill for Carl Johnson.

As the invasion date neared, the missions became more dangerous. On 12 August, the Group lost six pilots to flak. George Rhodes downed a Bf 109 during the same mission. Despite the steady stream of losses, the Group continued to undertake simultaneous missions on many days, including escorts to Ploesti. On 23 August the 332nd formation was intercepted by seven fighters, one of which was downed by Luke Weathers and William Hill. On 24 August three more enemy fighters were destroyed by John Briggs, William Thomas and Charles McGee.

On 25 August the Group returned to Ploesti, losing one aircraft to engine trouble. During an escort mission for B-24s on 27 August the returning 'Red Tails' destroyed 22 aircraft as they strafed two enemy airfields. A dedicated strafing mission against an airfield in Rumania on 30 August saw the 332nd destroy 83 more German aircraft on the ground.

September's bad weather saw the Group perform only 16 missions, mainly bomber escorts, but including a strafing mission against Ilandza, in Yugoslavia, which left 36 enemy aircraft burning. The weather broke in October, and attacks on targets in Greece began in earnest before the Allied invasion. Attacks on Greek airfields were costly and relatively ineffective, claiming the lives of several Tuskegee pilots, but with few enemy aircraft destroyed. On 4 October five enemy aircraft fell before the guns of George Gray, George Rhodes, Edward Thomas and Shelby Westbrook, with Henry Perry and Milton Hayes sharing a kill. Elements of the Group undertook a sweep from Budapest to Bratislava on 11 October. Only 20 of the 72 P-51 s that took off were able to find gaps in the cloud, but these aircraft attacked river traffic on the Danube, and strafed three airfields, on which they destroyed 17 enemy aircraft.

On 12 October, while returning from escorting bombers, the 302nd FS destroyed nine aircraft in the air while the 99th, 301st and 302nd accounted for 26 on the ground. The aerial victories were credited to Milton Brooks, William Green, Wendell Pruitt (two), Luther Smith and Roger Romine, with the remaining three falling before the guns of Lee Archer.

Because the last of these brought Archer's score to five, his first kill (dating from July) was re-examined, and officially re-evaluated as a shared kill! To make matters worse, Archer had to land on the island of Vis to refuel on the way home, damaging his propeller when he ran off the PSP runway. October was generally not a good month for the 332nd, however, the unit losing 15 pilots.

Lt Charles McGee (left) and his crewchief pose in front of 'their' P-51C, *KITTEN*. The former was attached to the 302nd FS, and claimed a kill on 24 August 1944 whilst on a bomber escort to Ploesti. A career officer, McGee later flew F-51Ds (again christened *KITTEN*) during the Korea War and RF-4C Phantom IIs over Vietnam

The 'Red Tails' became increasingly popular with bomber crews, who soon noticed that when they were under the protection of the 332nd FG there were no losses to enemy fighters. 'The P-38s always stayed way out, we couldn't tell if they were friend or foe and they were too far out to do any good. Some of the other Mustang groups stayed in too close, and if we were attacked it would be over before they could do anything to protect us. With other groups, we got the feeling that they just wanted to go and shoot down 109s, and didn't care if they left us to it. The "Red Tails" were always out there where we thought they should be. We were very comfortable with the "Red Tails"; we thought they were the best fighter escort we could get. We had no idea they were black – it was the army's best kept secret!', remembered one B-24 pilot.

A particular boost to bomber crews' morale was the 'Red Tail's' practise of detaching aircraft to escort damaged stragglers. On 16 November, three P-51s flown by Melvin Jackson, Louis Purnell and Luke Weathers were escorting a crippled bomber when they were bounced by eight Bf 109s. Luke Weathers downed two of these to score the only aerial victories of the month. He remembers the engagement to this day:

'Col Davis detailed me, along with 'Red' Jackson and Louis Purnell to escort a B-24 with two engines out. I located the bomber and headed to make the intercept. It was a beautiful day with ceiling and visibility unlimited. I slid in on the shaded side of the bomber, reduced the throttle setting and settled down for a peaceful ride home. The sun warmed the cockpit making me drowsy, and the oxygen from my mask didn't seem to help. Scanning the sky I spotted aircraft at two o'clock high but too far away to be identified. Jackson and Purnell went to investigate, and soon called eight Bf 109s in two flights of four. Not knowing where they were, I waited in the shadow of the bomber. My best bet would be to stop the string attack they were known to use on crippled bombers and isolated fighters. The Bf 109s changed from box formation to string. I waited in the shadow of the bomber and watched as the string of German fighters headed towards us. I had no choice but to stand and fight. My heart beat increased, faster and louder becoming an inner voice saying "Wait, not now. Now – go".

'I dropped my wing tanks and turned into the German formation just as the lead Bf 109 dropped his nose to start his attack. I gave him a burst with my .50 cals, then fanned the rudder left and right to spray the rest of the formation. The lead Bf 109 nosed up, smoke from the engine engulfing the cockpit. He turned over and went spinning towards the ground, and the German formation broke up. I rolled over on my back and pulled back, following the smoking Bf 109 as it hurtled towards the ground. Calling on the radio I asked Jackson and Purnell where they were, and the

Luke Weathers sits on the wing of his second Mustang, named *Beale Street*, surrounded by a motley selection of crew chiefs – judging by all the B-6 'bomber jackets' in evidence, this shot was taken in the early winter months of 1945

latter answered "right behind you". I relaxed and levelled off, but something wasn't right.

'I turned slightly to look behind and all I could see was a cannon in the centre of the spinner of the aircraft behind me. It wasn't Purnell – I had a Bf 109 on my tail. I dropped flaps and chopped the throttle at the same time. Old *Beale Street* hung in space, the Bf 109 passed underneath and I was on his tail. A few short bursts for range and the 109 turned, too late. One long burst and the cockpit and left wing disintegrated. Two more 109s were still in range, and easy prey, but the voice of Col Davis rang loud and clear in my mind. "Your job is to protect the bombers and not to chase enemy aircraft for personal glory". I headed back to the bomber.'

Twenty-two missions were flown during December. The Group escorted bombers to Brux, Germany, on Christmas Day, but the four Bf 109s encountered were not attacked. By the end of 1944 the Group's tally stood at 62 confirmed air-to-air victories. January was not a busy month, with the Group flying only 11 missions, mainly bomber and reconnaissance escorts. More missions were planned and briefed, but were scrubbed in the face of inclement weather. February was a busier month with 39 missions flown. During a fighter sweep to Munich Lt William S Price shot down a Bf 109, the first aerial victory of 1945, although enemy air activity was otherwise negligible. Davis himself led the Group on its 200th mission on 28 February, covering the B-17s of the 5th BW as they attacked Verona.

Lt S L Curtis is strapped in and ready for his next escort mission from Ramitelli. The complex canopy framing and generally cluttered cockpit area associated with the P-51B/C is clearly visible in this shot. Like other FGs in Italy, the 332nd flew the early model Mustang into 1945

The output of black pilots from Tuskegee was never sufficient to supply enough replacements for the 332nd FG, meaning that pilots tended to have to undertake longer tours of duty than men in other units. 332nd pilots could quite easily clock up 125 missions in a tour (50 was the theatre-wide length of tour, officially). The growing requirement for pilots for the new Negro-manned 477th BG put further pressure on an already stretched system. The 332nd FG's fourth unit inactivated in early March.

On 24 March 1945, Col Davis led 59 of the Group's aircraft on the longest escort mission ever flown by the Fifteenth Air Force, covering B-17s as they bombed the Daimler Benz tank works in Berlin (a 1600-mile round trip). The Group earned a Distinguished Unit Citation for 'outstanding performance and extraordinary heroism', not least for carrying on to the target when the group which should have relieved them failed to show up at the rendezvous on the outskirts of Berlin!

As the 332nd FG's pilots recalculated their fuel figures, German jets started to appear over the capital. Me 262s were not often encountered by Fifteenth Air Force fighters, although intelligence reports had indicated that the type was active in the fighter role, and that its performance would outclass that of the P-51. Such worries were proved to be groundless, since the Me 262s were in the main poorly flown, and were not unbeatable. The 332nd FG proved this over Berlin, when three jets fell to Lt Roscoe C Browne, Lt Robert W Williams and Lt Samuel Watts. Two more, and a single Me 163 rocket fighter, were claimed as probables, and three Me 262s were damaged. Three 'Red Tail' pilots were shot down on the mission, however.

On 31 March 46 Mustangs undertook a sweep of the Munich area, with rail targets nominated as a priority. The mission resulted in the destruction of seven locomotives and 16 enemy fighters. Five Bf 109s and an Fw 190 were destroyed in an initial encounter, while the 100th destroyed ten of a the eight Fw 190s and three Bf 109s that engaged them five minutes later. Lt Robert Williams claimed two of the Fw 190s, with five more destroyed by Rual Bell, Thomas Braswell, Roscoe Brown, John Lyle and Bertram Wilson. Bf 109s were shot down by William Campbell, John Davis, James Hall, Earle Lane, Daniel Rich and Hugh White.

Twelve more enemy aircraft (eight Fw 190s and four Bf 109s) fell to the 332nd the following day after a hard fought dogfight that left three Mustangs destroyed and two Tuskegee pilots dead. The victorious 'Red Tail' pilots were Harry Stewart, with three kills, Charles White with two, Earl Carey and John Edwards, each with two, and Harold Morris, Walter Manning and James Fischer with one each. Lt Jimmy Lanham shot down a lone Bf 109 on 5 April.

On 15 April, Ben Davis led a strafing mission against rail traffic in Austria, destroying 35 locomotives, 52 other rail vehicles, four barges and four trucks. A single enemy fighter was also shot down. Col Davis won himself a Silver Star in the process. The Group finished its scoring on 26 April, claiming what were to be the last kills in the Mediterranean theatre. Six 'Red Tailed' Mustangs escorting a recce P-38 to Linz were bounced by five Bf 109s. Four were claimed as kills, the fifth falling as a probable. Jimmy Lanham received one victory credit and the probable, while Thomas Jefferson gained two credits.

The Group flew the last of its 9152 sorties for the Fifteenth Air Force on 30 April 1945, these being additional to 6381 sorties flown by the 99th FS with the Twelfth Air Force. The Group had destroyed 111 enemy aircraft in the air and another 150 on the ground, and other targets included a destroyer sunk by gunfire! A total of 66 Tuskegee pilots were killed in action. The Group ended the war at Cattolica in preparation for the final offensive against Germany, but this was forestalled by the unconditional surrender on 7 May. For a time it looked as though the 332nd might have to ship out to the Far East for the continuing war against Japan, before the two atomic bombs brought the war to a close.

When the conflict was over, the Tuskegee airmen returned home to a segregated America. Remarkably, many pilots chose to stay in the USAAF, and saw the desegregation of the force, perhaps due to their outstanding example. Adding to the laurels they had won in World War 2, the 332nd FG won the prestigious Air Force National Fighter Gunnery Meet of 1949. One of the team members, Harry Stewart, had already demonstrated his gunnery skills some four years earlier over Germany when he despatched three Bf 109s in short order!

Lt Willard Woods has adorned his Mustang with an Ace of Clubs immediately below the cockpit. A crude 'ring and bead' sight can just be seen affixed to the windscreen framing directly in the pilot's eyeline

Col Davis and an unknown officer from the 99th FS have an informal chat with two crewchiefs from the squadron at Ramitelli in late 1944

THE 354TH FG

Although it was by no means the first Mustang unit to see operational service – this honour surely rests with the RAF – the 354th FG adopted the name 'Pioneer' because it was the first to take the Merlin-engined P-51B into frontline combat. It could also be argued that this statement is only accurate if further qualified by calendar dates marking the commencement of operations, but it remained a semi-official title, which probably appeased anyone with a more legitimate claim!

Cast into an administrative and publicity 'limbo' as a tactical Group flying strategic missions until such times as the Eighth's own fighter units could be re-equipped with Mustangs, the 'Pioneers', led by Col Kenneth R Martin, simply got on with the job. Assigned pilots forgot the awesome responsibility they had been given, and revelled in flying the P-51B. What they could not at times overlook was the fact that this thoroughbred needed breaking-in before it could become a true winner, and in this respect too they were 'pioneers' in more senses than one.

The pilots had a good tutor in the redoubtable Don Blakeslee, boss of the famed 4th FG 'Eagles' at Debden, in Essex. Under his no-compromise guidance, the 354th emerged as a highly professional outfit, more than fit to pave the way for the safe shepherding of the heavy bombers to any point where the Germans maintained a factory, an airfield, a railhead or myriad other installations important to their war effort.

As they prepared for their combat debut, 354th FG pilots realised that in their hands rested the practicality of continuing long-range fighter escort, and for a few weeks the 'Pioneers' would handle that challenge alone. No pilots had actually been trained to withstand the rigours of six to seven-hour stints in the cramped confines of a fighter cockpit, and it is not overstressing the case to say that had the 354th failed in its task, or had the P-51B not measured up as well as it did, the US bombing campaign would have had to have been drastically revised.

That the 'Pioneers' undertook the escort role as well as, if not better than, any other group in the ETO has tended perhaps to be overlooked in

Wearing freshly-applied white theatre markings adopted by the 354th FG soon after they went operational in the ETO in late 1943, this early-build P-51B 'GQ'-coded machine hails from the 355th FS (*via Phil Jarrett*)

the official grouping of the Eighth and Ninth Air Force units, and the cross-over nature of its operations for some eight months until D-Day.

Formed in January 1943 at Tonopah, Nevada, the 354th comprised the 353rd, 355th and 356th FSs. Equipped with P-39s immediately before being alerted to move to England in November 1943, the Group's pilots felt confident enough to fly almost anything in combat. Rumours amongst the pilots that they were to receive Merlin-powered P-51s once in England were rife, but being a new and untried type, it was more realistic to believe the scuttlebutt that the Group would have to 'sweat it out' with hand-me-down fighters, at least for a short period of time.

Although the ground echelon arrived at Boxted, in Essex (the aerodrome assigned to the Group in the ETO), the pilots found themselves at Greenham Common, in Berkshire. P-51As hastily borrowed from the 10th RG helped them complete the ETO check-out process, and a week later the entire Group was overjoyed to find that brand new P-51Bs had indeed arrived at Boxted. In-theatre training lasted a month, and by 1 December 1943 the 354th was deemed combat-ready. Col Don Blakeslee duly led a force of 24 P-51Bs over St Omer for his 'flock' to watch the flak coming up, and apart from a few holes, they suffered no mishaps.

Low over the North Sea, a 356th FS P-51B named *CISCO* shows to advantage the white stripes applied to the wings and tailplane, as well as the nose and fin

Blakeslee went on to lead more missions, and on 13 December the enemy was encountered by the 354th for the first time. A 'probable' was the only claim, but one P-51B was lost to causes unknown. The rookie ETO pilots, noting Blakeslee's sound, but uncompromising, pep talks, wondered who they feared most, him or the Luftwaffe.

Among Blakeslee's simplified edicts was that the 354th's pilots should strive to shoot down enemy fighters or be shot down themselves; 'make', he said, 'the enemy pilot voluntarily break off his attack first and failing all else, you should maintain a collision course with individual enemy fighters, particularly those which appear more enthusiastic than their fellows about shooting down heavy bombers'. The veteran 4th FG boss meant this last piece of advice, for as dangerous as it sounded, it was invariably the case that the opposing pilot would lose his nerve first, initiate the break and thus set himself up as a target for a few vital seconds. And most of the time, it worked.

Winter missions demonstrated all too clearly the additional meteorological hazards the 354th was to face in the ETO. Pilots used to flying in clear visibility in the US found themselves climbing on instruments through 'pea soup' English fog, not daring to deviate for fear of collision, until breaking out into sunny skies. New skills had to be learned quickly.

In common with other US fighter groups which based their operational procedures on those of the RAF, the 'Pioneers' divided its three squadrons into A, B, C and D Flights of four Mustangs each. These designations were permanent, while the flight colours – Red, White, Blue and Green – were rotated. 'Red' Flight was usually led by the squadron commander, while the sought-after 'Green' Flight – the one considered the most flexible as it was assigned to range out ahead of the formation and take on any enemy flyers which challenged the bombers before the target was reached – was often the most effective in terms of aerial kills.

In the 354th, flight commanders were expected to lead two out of every three missions, the lead position on the remaining one being taken by another pilot so as to ensure that command experience was continually being gained by new pilots. This also meant that the flight could be capably led in the event of an emergency. For the 354th this system worked well, for at no time during combat was flight effectiveness reduced due to the loss of key personnel.

That the pilots had taken their training seriously was graphically demonstrated on the mission flown on 16 December, when the first enemy aircraft fell to the 354th's guns – from then on there was seemingly no stopping the 'Pioneers'. A mission to Kiel on 5 January 1944 proved the point. The group was briefed to provide withdrawal support for 'heavies' bombing targets in the city, but as the Mustangs approached the rendezvous point they came across a large gaggle of Luftwaffe fighters. American and German pilots became engaged in a series of dogfights, one of which involved 1st Lt Glenn Eagleston and an Fw 190.

Catching the *Jagdflieger* at 23,000 ft, Eagleston fired 35 rounds of ammo at his foe, using 45° of deflection. Whether or not his fire had been fatal was impossible to tell, but the enemy went into a full power dive with Eagleston in hot pursuit. Speed built up quickly to the point where the Focke-Wulf entered a violent spin from which the pilot could not recover. Glenn Eagleston felt elation as the Fw 190 crashed, thus marking his initial victory – the first of 18.5 aircraft that were to be credited to him.

The final total for the Kiel mission saw the 354th claim a highly respectable 'bag' of 18 enemy aircraft downed without loss. A week later came Maj Jim Howard's big day. A Medal of Honor was no mean achievement considering how few pilots had yet received America's top military decoration, and that fighter pilots, who were supposed to be the hunters and to exhibit natural aggressiveness, were not considered to be first in line for medals for simply doing their job. But those that were awarded to pilots flying fighters were invariably given for the accomplishment of exceptional deeds involving both skill and bravery. And Howard's six Bf 110s destroyed in a single mission (although he only claimed two confirmed and four probables, despite crewmembers of the beleaguered 401st BG stating they saw half-a-dozen Bf 110s go down during 30 minutes of solid dogfighting) surely fulfil both criterion.

On 11 January Col Martin led the 354th on an escort to Frankfurt at a stage of the war when the Luftwaffe could still deploy heavily-armed twin-engined fighters against the bombers with relative impunity – or so

The first Mustang ace in the ETO, then Maj Jim Howard was also the only fighter pilot in the theatre to win the Medal of Honor, awarded for his six-kill haul of 12 January 1944 – all Bf 110s, Howard only claimed two confirmed, however, despite independent witnesses from bombers in the vicinity of the action stating they saw all six *Zerstörers* shot down. By the time this shot was taken on 4 April 1944 Howard had been promoted to Lieutenant Colonel and given command of the 354th. His scoreboard also shows his six kills claimed against the Japanese in China whilst serving as a 'Flying Tiger' with the American Volunteer Group (AVG) in 1942 (*Fox Photo*)

its leaders thought. Long-range escort fighters were still something of an unknown quantity, and the Germans had little inkling as to how many there were in England. However, a number of crews were about to find out too late that even one group of P-51s was a big enough force to counter the instantly obsolete Messerschmitt 'twins'.

Consequently, 354th FG pilots met a German tactic that had been tried and tested. Bf 110s would make a pass at the bombers and dive away to escape the escort. Finding that the P-51s went after them, *Zerstörer* crews opted to make a fight of it. On this day they tried, and despite taking losses, nailed Martin and his wingman, Lt Richard McDonald. Martin, then with $4^{1}/_{2}$ kills, tested Blakeslee's dictum to the full by maintaining a collision course with a Bf 110. The German broke first, eye witnesses swore, only too late – P-51 and Bf 110 came together. Trying to protect his leader, McDonald was shot down by a second *Zerstörer*.

Jack Bradley was amongst the pilots involved in the melée. 'We saw an "Me 210" (Me 410) headed for a box of bombers and I went after him. He dove through an overcast to give the impression he was giving up the hunt, but we followed and kept an eye on him. He soon turned back

toward the bombers and we closed in and started pumping him. I saw the wheels go down and two of the crew ready to bail out.

'We climbed back and saw an Me 110 above us and to our left, ready to make a pass at the bombers. We took a steep climbing turn and caught right onto his tail. This time the Me's right engine started afire and I saw the canopy fall off and one man bail out. My guns then jammed and I went "upstairs" to direct the P-51s around me because I saw five Me 110s below and several Mustangs, but the clouds obstructed their view. I could see the enemy clearly from my position. First I directed (Don) Beerbower in an attack on an Me 110, and saw it dive into the ground. Then I radioed directions to (Edward) Fox who was in line for an Me 110, but because of cloud, could not see it well. I told him when to make the attack and when to hold fire. I watched this one go straight down in flames.'

Charles Gumm also participated in the decimation of the *Zerstörers* by

The nose of one of two P-51Bs flown by Jim Howard whilst CO of the 356th FS. It shows the rare, but not unique, combination of Japanese and German kill markings – as squadron boss, his aircraft was coded 'AJ-A'. The second P-51B at Howard's disposal at this time was identically marked, but was fitted with a Malcolm hood, one of the few such modified Mustangs issued to the 354th FG (*Crow*)

Texan Jack T Bradley's P-51B 43-6425 *MARGIE MARU* shows its impressive 15-kill scoreboard. Perhaps less well known than other fighter leaders in the ETO, he was nevertheless one of the most skilled, and among his other achievements Bradley helped to boost the confidence of pilots assigned to the ill-starred 363rd FG. He scored his first kill as early as 20 December 1943 whilst serving as Operations Officer within the 353rd FS, and had made ace by 20 February 1944. Bradley eventually assumed command of the unit in the spring of that year, and by the time he returned to the US on leave in August had raised his score to 14. He returned to combat in the autumn, when he was posted to the 354th's HQ flight as deputy commander, and assumed command of the Group early in 1945. Bradley's final kill was achieved on 23 March, his victim a lone Fw 190 (*Olmsted*)

Called 'executives' by the original AP caption writer, this photograph shows (left to right) Maj George Bickell, Lt Col Wallace B Mace and Maj Owen M Seaman of the 354th FG during the spring of 1944. The 354th's ETO exploits certainly warranted stories a bit later on, but the journalistic peg here was that all three pilots had been at Pearl Harbor on 7 December 1941 – although seasoned campaigners, none made ace – Bickell did claim 3.5 kills in P-51B 43-12173 *"Peg O'my Heart"*, parked behind them in this shot, however

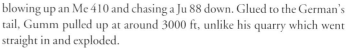

blowing up an Me 410 and chasing a Ju 88 down. Glued to the German's tail, Gumm pulled up at around 3000 ft, unlike his quarry which went straight in and exploded.

Among the characters who flew with the 'Pioneers' was Wau Kau Kong, a Chinese national who hailed from Honolulu – he also scored a Fw 190 on the 11 February mission. The Boxted Group's tally continued to mount to the point where it began to rival the successes of Hubert Zemke's famed P-47-equipped 56th FG. The 354th's pilots set themselves the challenge of bettering the 'Wolfpack's' scoring rate, and by late February this had been achieved through the claiming of 103 enemy aircraft in 83 days of combat – the 100th kill for the Group fell to Bob Stephens, who finished the war with a total of 13 victories.

With Jim Howard (the 354th's first ace following his Bf 110 kill on 30 January) having replaced Martin as Group CO, the gruelling pace set by the former boss did not slacken, but there were moments of light relief such as when Clayton Gross came home to claim 12 Nazi telephone conversations probably destroyed. Gross had landed at Boxted with a yard of high tension cable wrapped around his fuselage, a souvenir from hedge-hopping around Lille. Seeing six Fw 190s about to land at an airfield and deciding he was outnumbered, Gross got the hell out, ripping through the telephone lines as he went.

There were other unusual things about the 354th, like enlisted pilots – Sgts Richards, Johns, Ferguson, Dempsey and Aney, all of whom had served initially with the RAF/RCAF. All flew combat missions before their commissions came through – strictly against regulations – and with Howard's blessing. Ignoring red tape, Howard knew men who had flown Spitfires in combat with the Commonwealth forces could make a valuable contribution to the group.

Tragedy always waited on the sidelines of an operational fighter station, and the 354th experienced a sad loss on 1 March 1944. Lt Charles Gumm, by then the Group's leading aces with six kills, took up a P-51B for a routine air test, and when his engine failed, instead of bailing out he rode the Mustang down to avoid it crashing into a crowded English village. He almost made it until one wing hit a tree, forcing the stricken fighter to cartwheel and explode. Gumm was thrown out and killed instantly.

Escorts and sweeps continued from Boxted until a base move came on 17 April to Maidstone, in Kent. There, the 'Pioneers' found instead of concrete hardstands and permanent RAF-style hangars and living quarters, Nissen huts, tents and PSP strip laid over grass.

Any gripes about such deprivation tended to be dispelled by anticipation of the cross-Channel invasion. In preparation for almost total Allied command of the air over the Normandy landing beaches, the 354th reverted back to its tactical role and joined dozens of other squadrons in the dive-bombing and strafing of German targets many miles inland from the coastal areas which would be vital to hold in the early hours of *Overlord*. The pace was hectic, the Group flying missions on both 3 and 4 June, but it was not required on D-Day itself. After the 6th, the 354th began the demanding task of escorting C-47 transports and their glider trains. Escort work was always exacting, but a laden Skytrain lumbered

Capt Felix Rogers admires the freshly-applied nose art on his P-51B 43-12161. A member of the high-scoring 353rd FS, Rogers was one of three pilots from the unit to finish with 7 kills at war's end

P-51B 43-6322 was named *The Verna Q* and *Stinky* by its regular pilot, Capt Frank Q O'Connor, who scored 10.75 kills whilst serving with the 356th FS. This aircraft was the first of a trio of similarly-named Mustangs flown by O'Connor during the course of his combat career, the latter two being P-51Ds (*Crow*)

along even slower than a bombed-up B-17, and the pilots were not unhappy when this gruelling phase of operations was finally over.

On 13 June the 354th left not only the jurisdiction of the Eighth AAF, but England itself. Alerted to move to France, the 'Pioneers' now found themselves as part of the 100th Fighter Wing, XIX Tactical Air Command, under the leadership of Brig Gen O P Weyland. The landing ground A-2 at Criqueville, near Grand-Camp-les-Baines on the Normandy coast, was the 354th's new home from 23 June, and from this base pilots flew a succession of escorts for B-26 formations, fighter sweeps, dive-bombing missions, close support and armed recon sorties.

On 4 July Gen Eisenhower visited A-2. As the Supreme Allied Commander for *Overlord*, 'Ike' wanted to observe from the air the progress of the fighting in the St Lo area, flying as a passenger in a P-51B the 354th had converted into a two-seater 'in the field'. Gen 'Pete' Queseda of IX Tactical Air Command led the sortie, and the 356th FS flew escort. 'Ike' squeezed into the bucket seat behind the pilot of the P-51B and unconcernedly watched the groundcrew screw down the Plexiglas side panels.

The Mustang conversion had left no room for a parachute to be worn by the rear-seat occupant, and had it been shot down 'Ike' would have had less than an even chance of survival – small wonder that Richard Turner, who then commanded the 356th, got next to no sleep the previous night.

Under strict radio silence lest the Germans got wind of the fact that they could have neutralised the most important general the Allies had, the mission got underway. In the event, Eisenhower was delighted with his flight, although Turner himself regretted flying a new P-51D on the sortie. Unbeknown to him, a pressure-sensing line had not been connected to the oil pressure gauge, giving a 'zero' reading. Turner had little choice but to return to Criqueville without a word over the radio, but he swore thereafter to always fly his own assigned aircraft.

Four days after the top brass visit, the 355th FS engaged a large formation of Bf 109s and Fw 190s. On a routine frontline patrol to the St Lo area, two P-51 flights led by Lt Col Lowell K Brueland had reached almost the limit of their fuel after an uneventful sortie. Suddenly, a large flight of German fighters was reported heading for the frontline and the 355th was ordered to intercept. Forty-plus Bf 109s materialised at high altitude, as did 20 Fw 190 *Jabos* lower down. Initially, all the Mustangs quickly climbed to engage the Messerschmitts and break up their formation, Brueland himself claiming two downed.

Then one flight of four, again led

by Brueland, went after the Focke-Wulfs. The Mustangs' fire forced the German pilots to jettison their bombs, and in the ensuing dogfights the Lieutenant-Colonel destroyed one, probably got a second and damaged a third. All told the P-51s shot down 12 Bf 109s and Fw 190s.

A second base move was made on 13 August when the 'Pioneers' set up shop at A-31 at Gael, near Montfort; on the 16th the P-51s were involved in two separate engagements with the Luftwaffe, the 16 aircraft involved claiming 13-0-2 for the loss of four of their own. Operations in support of the Allied push continued until the 25th, when the 'Pioneers' ran into Bf 109s and Fw 190s, and a running battle took place over Rethel, Reims and Beauvais. US claims were 36-1-8 in the air, and this was followed by a successful attack on Beauvais airfield, near Reims, which caught an Fw 190 unit in the act of refuelling. The strafing P-51s destroyed more than a dozen fighters without loss, an operation for which the 354th was awarded a second Distinguished Unit Citation.

Then on 17 September it was another move, to Orconte and ALG A-66, near St Dizier, a base occupied until 1 December when the 354th began operating from A-98 near Roiseres-en-Haye. While it was at A-98

Then Maj Richard Turner was one of the 40-plus aces that made the 354th the top scoring fighter outfit in the ETO by war's end. This is a view of him in his P-51B with but a modest four kills recorded. The swastikas would later number 21, 11 of which were aerial victories. Second-ranking ace of the 356th FS, Turner was a close friend of Jim Howard's during their time together in the 354th, taking over the latter's squadron after Howard was promoted to Lieutenant Colonel *(Crow)*

the 'Pioneer Mustang Group' was informed that it was soon to convert to the P-47! This move, made by the top brass in the interests of Ninth AAF standardisation, was understandably received with little enthusiasm. To pilots thoroughly schooled in the P-51, the prospect of saddling up the mighty Thunderbolt seemed a retrograde step. Good aircraft though the P-47 was, it was a far heavier machine to fly when compared with the agile Mustang, and few pilots were convinced that the change was for the best.

Orders were complied with, however, and the Group duly flew Thunderbolts during the worst winter months of 1944/45. Beforehand, on 5 November, the 'Pioneers' strafed three German airfields and claimed 28-1-16, and on the 17th the Mustangs hit Zellhausen airfield, leaving a further 15 aircraft in flames in a fitting swansong to the Group's initial P-51 phase. It was a little ironic that some of the 354th's now-surplus Mustangs were passed on to the Ninth WRS, which proceeded to fly the secondhand fighters on weather search missions, complete with 354th FG markings on their noses.

With the final German land offensive in the West contained by the spring of 1945, the 354th's Thunderbolts helped maintain the pressure until on 16 February pilots were heartened to hear that their P-51s were

Lt Col Dick Turner's last P-51D (44-63672/'AJ-T') is used as a backdrop for his dedicated groundcrew at the 356th FS. The abbreviated name came about as a result of Turner receiving a 'Dear John' letter to say that 'Sallee' had transferred her affections elsewhere – so her name came of the 'ship', pronto! This aircraft passed to Capt McIntyre and was renamed *Shanty Irishman* following Turner's rotation home *(Crow)*

to be returned. With renewed zeal, the 354th henceforth set about supporting the last phases of the war in Europe, flying less colourful Mustangs than previously seen, the stars, triangles and diamonds of the immediate pre-P-47 period having given way to plain coloured spinners and nose bands.

Pilots, glad to be flying what they viewed to be the best fighter again, also found the enemy active, to the satisfaction of those who had either been posted to the 354th in 1945, or who had yet to open their scores.

The P-51D assigned to Lt 'Moe' Stach became a little uglier than the pilot reckoned with soon after he set out on this mission – whether or not Moe was flying it at the time is unknown. A ground-flip like this could cause the pilot fatal injuries as that big canopy tended to stick way up proud of the fuselage spine, and if the tail broke off (as it appears to have done here), it was that much nearer the ground. Luckily, this kind of accident was relatively rare (*Olmsted*)

Unusually, this anonymous 353rd FS pilot has turned his victory tally – in the form of small aircraft silhouettes – almost into a squadron marking by painting them on the fin of his P-51D. A question arises as to why *Wiggle's Papa* had three symbols under the cockpit and four on the fin when seen at Toul, France, in 1944 (*Crow*)

Bob Ramer's well-decorated P-51D 44-63668 of the 355th FS, seen on a German airfield near the end of the war. Eight-and-a-half kills (Ramer's final total) are painted under the cockpit, the USAAF following the RAF practice of allocating percentage shares in enemy aircraft kills. This P-51 had originally been six-kill ace Capt Clayton Gross's *Live Bait*, and the story goes that Ramer 'acquired' it whilst the former was briefly home on leave, renamed it *ENSIGN BABS*, and was shot down in it over Germany – all whilst Gross was back in America. Rumour has it that the aircraft's former owner was far from impressed to learn of these goings on upon his return, and has never forgiven Ramer to this day!

One pilot who almost left it too late to increase his tally was Lt Bruce Carr. Having shot down 6.5 enemy aircraft, he had taken leave during the 354th's P-47 period, but by the time he returned the Luftwaffe was apparently shattered and rarely appeared in strength. It did so on 2 April, however, and Carr waded into the flock of Bf 109s and Fw 190s encountered over Naumberg, despatching three Focke-Wulfs and two Messerschmitts to make him the Ninth's sole official 'ace in a day'. By war's end Carr's score had rocketed to 14 victories, thus making him the fourth-ranking 354th ace after Eagleston, Beerbower and Bradley.

Flying from A-98 until 8 April, the 354th occupied Ober Ulm (Y-64) and three weeks later, was flying from R-45 at Ansbach, the latter turning

The *Prodigal Son* was flown by Bartholomew Tenore of the 356th FS, who is credited with 6 kills, some of which must have been strafing claims as his name fails to appear in contemporary USAAF aces listings (*Olmsted*)

Lt Bruce Carr's P-51D is bombed up for one of its final forays over the remains of the Third Reich in 1945. As befitting a tactical fighter unit, the 354th eventually integrated fully into Ninth Air Force air support operations after a successful stint on long-range escort with the Eighth Air Force. To have scored so many aerial victories in so short a time was an outstanding achievement. Carr's final score of 14 made him the fourth-ranking 354th ace, and within this tally was a single day's haul of five (three Fw 190s and two Bf 109s) kills scored on 2 April 1945

Lt Col Glenn T Eagleston's P-51D at Herzogenauach, Germany, in 1945, with 23.5 kills painted on – a score that made him the top-ranking ace in the 354th. His aircraft carried no name, but with a surname like his, what other decoration could Eagleston use? A rendering similar to this had earlier appeared on his P-47D. The pilot striking a pose in front of his CO's aircraft is Lt Cary Salter, Jr (*Crow*)

out to be the Group's final European base. After April, sortie levels reduced significantly as targets still impeding the Allied armies were far more scarce. But German jets represented a challenge to P-51 pilots, and one that they were eager to test. Capt Clayton K Gross took up the gauntlet on 14 April while leading a flight on a sweep over the River Elbe. He duly returned to base with an Me 262 kill confirmed.

On 8 May 1945 the 354th's 17 months of combat came to an end; during that time it had despatched 18,334 Mustang and Thunderbolt sorties on 1834 separate missions. The Group had also produced at least 41 aces and other top rate pilots who contributed to the destruction of 701 enemy aircraft in aerial combat, thus making the 354th the highest scoring fighter group in the ETO. Their ace list was also considerably longer than that achieved by any other group in either the Eighth, Ninth or Fifteenth AAFs.

For the loss of 187 pilots killed, or missing in action, the 354th FG therefore turned in a combat ratio of 3.74 victories for every man lost. The 353rd FS was the top scorer on P-51s with 276.50 victories out of a total of 289.50 (which included 13 kills on P-47s), 84 pilots sharing in the score. For comparison, the second and third highest-scoring squadrons in the ETO were both bomber-escort optimised Eighth AAF units – the 357th's 364th FS with 212 victories shared by 70 pilots coming second, and the 352nd's 487th FS with 206 kills by 62 pilots placed third.

1

P-51D-5-NA (NA.109) 44-13383 *Swede's Steed III* of 1st Lt William Y 'Swede' Anderson, 353rd FS/354th FG, Ninth AAF

Anderson named each of his Mustangs *Swede's Steed*. The third steed was this P-51D-5-NA. Soon after the eighth kill marking was applied the aircraft was modified with a dorsal fin fillet. The yellow spinner and nose band, with dark blue triangles superimposed, was an unofficial unit recognition device applied as the 354th FG decamped to France in the wake of the invasion. A prancing horse insignia was applied to the tail in orange.

2

P-51B-1-NA (NA.102) 43-12375 *BONNIE "B" II* of Capt Donald M 'Buzz' Beerbower, 353rd FS/354th FG, Ninth AAF

Beerbower's second named aircraft was a Malcolm-hooded B. Seen here with 15 kill markings, *BONNIE "B" II* had full D-Day stripes, the overlap between these being grey. The yellow nose has not yet had its triangles applied, an omission pre-dating the unit markings adopted after the 353rd's brief P-47 interlude. The white fin and rudder recognition band was removed following an order dated 23 March 1944, but white wing and tailplane bands were retained, as were the black fin bands applied to natural metal aircraft.

3

P-51D-5-NA (NA.109) 44-13628 *BONNIE B III* of Capt Donald M 'Buzz' Beerbower, CO 353rd FS/354th FG, Ninth AAF

When other long-serving pilots were rotated home, Beerbower stayed behind as CO of the 353rd FS. Downed by flak on 9 August 1944, he was leading scorer of the 354th FG with 15.5 kills at the time of his death, and was duly awarded a posthumous DSC. When the 353rd FS replaced its white (black on natural metal aircraft) nose bands and spinners, it initially applied a yellow spinner only – this colour was later extended over the nose band, with a saw-tooth of black or dark blue triangles pointing forward. The P-51 has partial D-Day stripes, these having been removed from upper surfaces of USAAF aircraft in late July 1944.

4

P-51D-5-NA (NA.109) 44-13693 *Angel's Playmate* of Capt Bruce W Carr, 353rd FS/354th FG, Ninth AAF

Carr was transferred to the 353rd FS from the 363rd FG while facing a court martial for insubordination, having caused problems with his over aggressiveness in the air and rebelliousness on the ground. These qualities were recognised as being potentially useful by Glenn Eagleston, who arranged for Carr's transfer. The latter ended the war with 14 confirmed air-to-air victories, 3 more unconfirmed, and 11 strafing kills. Unusually, Carr's second-last aircraft had dark blue triangles on its yellow nose band – the marking used by the unit before it traded its P-51s for P-47s, but generally replaced by a simple yellow band and spinner after the squadron regained Mustangs. Carr's replacement *Angel's Playmate*, 44-63497, received in April 1945, was almost identical, but had the plain yellow nose. Fourth overall in the Ninth's air-to-air scoring table, Carr's 11 strafing victories made him the top overall ace of this AAF.

5

P-51B-10-NA (NA.104) 42-106602 *SHELLELAGH* of Capt Kenneth H Dahlberg, 353rd FS/354th FG, Ninth AAF

Although he was one of the 353rd's top-scorers, Dahlberg was not allocated a P-51 of his own, and today denies that he ever flew an aircraft named *'Dahlberg's Dilemma'* as has been reported elsewhere. Other aircraft flown by Dahlberg included *Little Horse* and Rogers' *Beantown Banshee*. He also flew two aircraft named after the traditional Irish weapon. Both were Malcolm-hooded P-51Bs, and were similarly marked. This *SHELLELAGH* had originally been delivered in olive drab finish, and had been stripped to natural metal. The other similarly-named aircraft had *SHELLELAGH* superimposed on a stylised club, and had D-Day stripes and camouflaged top decking and upper-surfaces. The regular pilots of these P-51s remain unknown.

6

P-51D-20-NA (NA.122) 44-63607 of Lt Col Glenn T Eagleston, CO 353rd FS/354th FG, Ninth AAF

Eagleston used a succession of similarly marked P-51s, the last of which wore $23^1/2$ kill symbols, although his official tally was only $18^1/2$.

7

P-51B-7-NA (NA.104) 43-6833 *Beantown Banshee* of Capt Felix M Rogers, 353rd FS/354th FG, Ninth AAF

Although *Beantown Banshee* was used by Ken Dahlberg to score some of his kills, it was one of two similarly-named P-51s regularly assigned to Felix 'Mike' Rogers, himself a seven-victory ace with the 353rd, and today the highest-ranking surviving Mustang ace. It has full D-Day stripes, and a yellow spinner provides the only unit identity beyond the 'FT' codes. The black nose ring is a vestige of the recognition markings applied to P-51s in the ETO. The aircraft is a rare P-51B-7-NA, with an extra 75 US gallon fuel tank in the fuse-

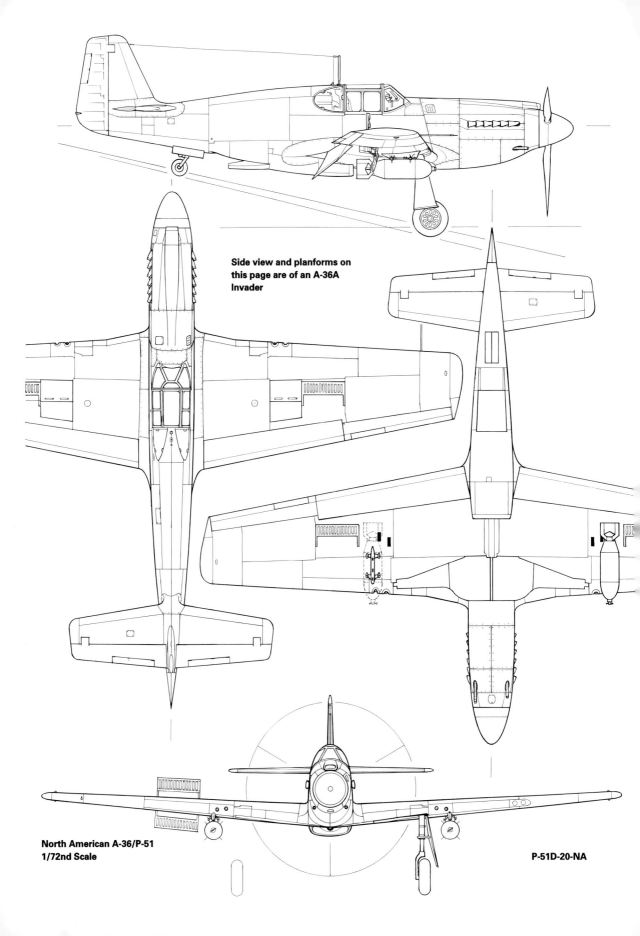

**Side view and planforms on
this page are of an A-36A
Invader**

**North American A-36/P-51
1/72nd Scale**

P-51D-20-NA

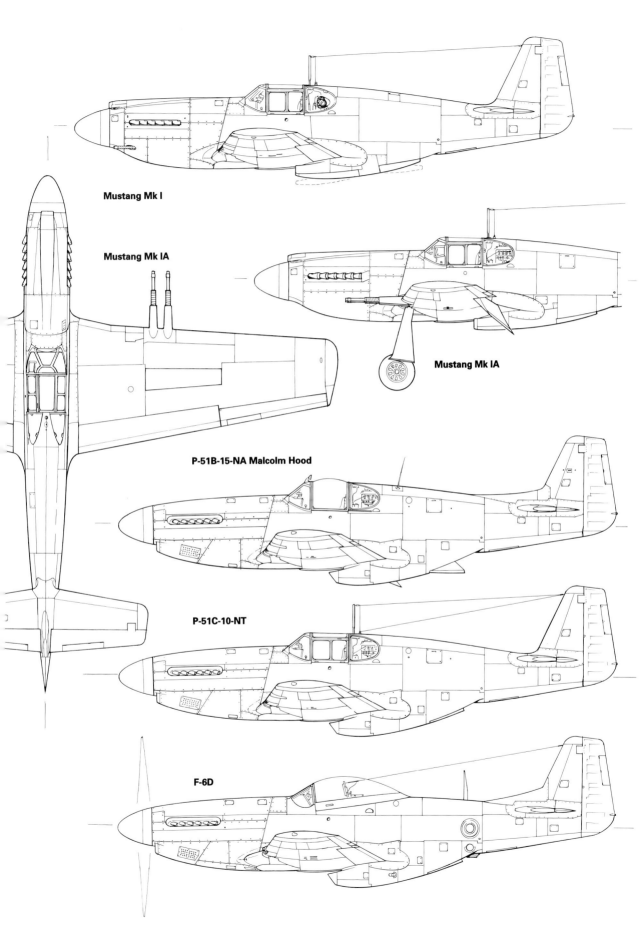

Mustang Mk I

Mustang Mk IA

Mustang Mk IA

P-51B-15-NA Malcolm Hood

P-51C-10-NT

F-6D

lage. This P-51B was amongst the first 769 delivered in olive drab and grey (43-7083 was the first sent from the factory unpainted). Only 200 P-51Cs were delivered camouflaged (up to 42-103178).

8

P-51B-1-NA (NA.102) 43-12173 *"Peg O'my Heart"* of 1st Lt George Bickell, 355th FS/354th FG, Ninth AAF

This P-51 wears an olive drab and neutral grey scheme, prior to the introduction of recognition markings designed to differentiate friend from foe. Unit identity codes were stencilled in white.

9

P-51D-20-NA (NA.122) 44-63702 *"Grim Reaper"* of Capt Lowell K Brueland, 355th FS/354th FG, Ninth AAF

Although Brueland remembers *'Wee Speck'* as being his long-term P-51, *"Grim Reaper"* carried 12 kill marks, representing most of his accredited 12$\frac{1}{2}$ aerial victories. White spinners and nose bands were replaced by blue or white spinners, with a blue and white checkered nose band.

10

P-51B-1-NA (NA.102) 43-12451 *LIVE BAIT* of Capt Clayton Gross, 355th FS/354th FG, Ninth AAF

This P-51 represents the typical early scheme worn by Mustangs in the ETO. It even retains the 12-inch horizontal white band across the fin and rudder, 18 inches below the fin tip. This feature was found to break up the outline of the P-51's fin, and it was ordered to be removed in March 1944 – no such order was made with respect to the black band applied to silver Mustangs in the same location, however. It carried the name *'Gwendolyn'* in small letters below the log of victories, with *LIVE BAIT* painted further forward. A later *LIVE BAIT* was natural-metal P-51D 44-63668, coded 'GQ-I'.

10A

P-51B-5-NA (NA.104) 43-6764 *Suga'* of Capt Charles W Lasko, 355th FS/354th FG, Ninth AAF

Seen in an early scheme, *Suga'* was used long enough by Lasko for it to don D-Day stripes, blue checkers on a white nose band and a Malcolm hood.

11

P-51B-5-NA (NA.104) 43-6315 *DING HAO!* of Maj James Howard, CO 356th FS/354th FG, Ninth AAF

Howard's second *DING HAO!* carried Japanese flags for his 6$\frac{1}{2}$ kills scored with the AVG, plus swastikas representing Luftwaffe victories.

12

P-51D-5-NA (NA.109) 44-13882 *UNO-WHO?* of Maj George 'Max' Lamb, 356th FS/354th FG, Ninth AAF

Credited with 7.5 P-51 kills, Lamb flew a series of P-51s named *UNO-WHO?* This one has the red

spinner and nose band introduced after the unit reconverted to Mustangs from the P-47 in 1945.

13

P-51B-5-NA (NA.104) 43-6322 *THE VERNA Q* of Maj Frank O'Connor, 356th FS/354th FG, Ninth AAF

O'Connor scored all of his 10.75 kills while flying with the 356th FS, taking command of the unit after Turner went home. His war ended when he was downed by flak after a diversionary attack on the guns. O'Connor bailed out, and was rescued from a civilian lynch mob by the *Wehrmacht*.

14

P-51B-I-NA (NA.102) 43-12434 *SHORT-FUSE SALLEE* of Capt Richard Turner, 356th FS/354th FG, Ninth AAF

Turner used at least five different P-51s during his two combat tours, and flew occasional sorties in other pilots' regular aircraft also. All his own machines wore a short-fused bomb on the nose, advertising his intended reaction if any enemy pilots messed with the bombers under his charge. Prior to his first tour, Turner had become virtually engaged to a girl named Sallee, and this was reflected in the name of his aircraft.

15

P-51D-15-NA (NA.109) 44-15622 "SHORT-FUSE" of Lt Col Richard Turner, CO 356th FS/354th FG, Ninth AAF

Turner took over the 356th FS when Jim Howard stepped down. He dropped the *'Sallee'* from his P-51 when he returned for his second tour, since relations with the young lady in question had mellowed! Following its P-47 phase, the unit's aircraft adopted new nose colours, wearing a red spinner and nose band in place of the blue star-spangled nose band and white (or blue) spinner. Despite the 19$\frac{1}{2}$ kill markings on the nose of this P-51, Turner was credited with only 11 aerial victories.

16

P-51D-5-NA (NA.109) 44-13706 *COURSER II* of Capt Morton A Kammerlohr, 380th FS/363rd FG, Ninth AAF

Kammerlohr replaced his P-51B 43-7194/'A9-I' with a P-51D – the former had worn the name *COURSER* in white on a blue arrow, while the second had *COURSER II* in red on the natural metal nose. Kammerlohr completed 76 missions and scored one kill – a Bf 109 on 28 May 1944. The 363rd flew fighter sorties from January 1944 until redesignated as a TRG in September. Escort missions featured during this period, but strafing and bombing sorties in support of the invasion were the priority – as a result pilots failed to score many victories.

17

P-51B-10-NA (NA.104) 42-106486 *Virginia* of Robert McGee, 382nd FS/363rd FG, Ninth AAF

Sharkmouths were rare on ETO P-51s during World War 2, but several 363rd FG machines were among the exceptions. McGee's *Virginia* and John Brown's *BIG MAC Junior* were similarly-marked with near-identical sharkmouths. The 363rd FG's three units (the 380th, 381st and 382nd) adopted blue, red and yellow spinners respectively as their colours following the move to France, having previously used black or white markings. Initially only the spinner was re-painted, with the nose band remaining in black or white according to whether the P-51 was natural metal or olive drab.

18

P-51B-5-NA (NA.104) 43-6438, *HOO FLUNG DUNG* of Maj Robert McWherter, 382nd FS/363rd FG, Ninth AAF

McWherter scored three kills with the 17th Provisional Squadron in the Pacific, before joining the 363rd. He was the top-scoring pilot to fly with the group. *HOO FLUNG DUNG*, named *CITY OF PARIS* on the starboard side, was an olive drab, Malcolm-hooded, P-51B.

19

P-51D-5-NA (NA.109) 44-13380 *HOO FLUNG DUNG* of Maj Robert McWherter, 382nd FS/363rd FG, Ninth AAF

Code-letters assigned to the 363rd FG were 'A9' for the 380th, 'B3' for the 381st and 'C3' for the 382nd FS. The units were re-designated as the 160th, 161st and 162nd TRSs in September 1944 when reassigned to the recce role. McWherter claimed three kills during his time with the 363rd, and three more in the Pacific (two of the latter were disallowed after the war). His P-51D was named in the same way as his B, with *City of Paris* to starboard.

20

P-51D-20-NA (NA.122) 44-63675, *Sierra Sue II* of Robert Bohna, 402nd FS/370th FG, Ninth AAF

Only a handful of pilots from the 370th FG scored aerial kills, not least because the unit operated almost exclusively in the fighter-bomber role for its brief existence with Mustangs from March until May 1945 – a period during which air opposition had disintegrated. *Sierra Sue II* survived to be sold to Sweden, and subsequently Nicaragua. Remarkably, it was then returned to the USA, and today flies in these colours over Minnesota.

21

P-51D-20-NA (NA.122) 44-63819 *KEEP SMILIN'* of Charles Nelson, 402nd FS/370th FG, Ninth AAF

The 402nd FS used blue as its colour, with a blue diagonal stripe on the fin and rudder and a blue nose. On some P-51s the colouring extended diagonally back in horizontal stripes to the wingroot. On these P-51s the anti-dazzle panel was also blue. Of the 370th FG's other units, the 401st used a yellow spinner and nose-band, with a yellow horizontal bar across fin and rudder, and the 485th used red nose markings and a red vertical stripe along the trailing edge of the fin ahead of the rudder.

22

F-6D, ex-P-51D-10-NA (NA.109) 44-14306 *Lil' Margaret* of Capt Clyde B East, 15th TRS/10th PRG, Ninth AAF

By war's end the Mustang formed the backbone of the USAAF's tactical recce force. The Ninth had three groups assigned; the 10th PRG, the 67th PRG and the 363rd TRG. The 111th TRS operated in the MTO, before joining the PRG of the 1st TAF, which became the 69th TRG in March 1945. These units scored a number of kills, and several produced aces. The most successful was the 10th TRS, which boasted no less than four aces, the leader, with 13 kills, being Clyde East. He had begun his flying career with No 414 Sqn, RCAF, flying Mustang Is, before transferring to the USAAF. East's F-6D wore the blue and white checkered tail top of the 10th PRG, with the blue and white checkered nose band of the 15th TRS. The 12th TRS used yellow and white checkers and the 162nd red and white.

23

F-6CNT ex-P-51C-5-NT 42-103368 of Capt John Hoefker, 15th TRS/10th PRG, Ninth AAF

East's greatest rival was John Hoefker, who flew this nameless F-6C for his first three kills from Chalgrove, in Oxfordshire. Visual recce missions were marked by binoculars, with photo-recce sorties marked by cameras. Five crosses represent Hoefker's aerial victories, a tally destined to reach 10$\frac{1}{2}$ kills. His later aircraft were similarly anonymous, including F-6D (44-14597/'SM-A') in which he was downed by flak on 23 December 1944. Hoefker bailed out, avoided capture and returned to his unit minus his boots, after a brief period in hospital for frostbitten feet.

24

A-36A-1-NA (NA.97) 42-83803 *PAT* of Lt Michael T Russo, 522nd FBS/27th FBG, Twelfth AAF

Russo was the Twelfth's only P-51A ace, and the only man to score five kills in an Allison-engined Mustang or Invader, period. Since the A-36 was a dedicated low-level attack aircraft, it is remarkable that the A-36 and P-51A units scored as many victories as they did. After his fifth kill Russo's A-36A had its code overpainted prior to the application of a short-lived skull and crossbones, and the legend 'Killer Russo', which covered the whole tailfin. This device was quickly removed, and the tailcode reinstated.

25

A-36A-1-NA (NA.97) 42-83901 *"Dorothy Helen"* of John P Crowder, 524th FBS/27th FBG, Twelfth AAF

John scored two kills while flying P-40s, but was not successful in the A-36. His aircraft was named *"Dorothy Helen"* after his wife. It originally carried its 'AA' code split by the fuselage star (in white on an insignia blue disc, without bars and bordered in yellow), with a 15-inch representation of 'Old Glory' on the tail. The red-bordered Type 3 national insignia was adopted in late June 1943, with a blue border replacing the red from September. On the A-36 the fuselage star was located well forward, but on the P-51A addition of bars flanking it forced the serial to be relocated to the tail. Yellow wing bands and a red spinner served as theatre markings, while some aircraft also had a diagonal white stripe across the fin/rudder. The yellow wing bands were 18 inches wide, and their outer edge was nine inches inboard from the aileron/flap intersection on the trailing edge.

26

P-51B-10-NA (NA.104) 42-106511 of Col Charles M McCorkle, CO 31st FG, Fifteenth AAF
It was the Group CO's prerogative to use his own initials instead of a conventional three-letter code, thus McCorkle had the codes 'CM-M' painted on his aircraft, repeating the letters 'CM' on the nose. The 31st FG otherwise used the same codes as the 78th FG in Britain, a deliberate duplication aimed at confusing the enemy. The 31st initially used a single diagonal red stripe as its marking, before five parallel diagonal stripes, covering the entire tailfin and rudder down to the top of the tailplanes, took its place. Although most P-51s delivered to the FG were natural metal finish, a handful were camouflaged, and these used white codes. The first P-51B/Cs in North Africa used the same yellow wing bands as the A-36s and P-51As, but with an additional span-wise band at the wingtip, and with a spanwise yellow band across each horizontal tailplane. McCorkle was already an ace when the 31st replaced its much-loved Spitfires Mk VIIIs with Mustangs. He scored six P-51 kills to add to the five he had scored on the Spitfire.

27

P-51D sub-type and serial unknown *Tempus Fugit* of Col Bill Daniel, CO 31st FG, Fifteenth AAF
Daniel's *Tempus Fugit* carries five kill markings and has the later style tail 'candy-striping' extending below the tailplanes over the lower fuselage. This P-51 has the later inboard yellow theatre band which quickly became standard. Its red rudder was a replacement scavenged from a damaged Mustang from another group, probably the 332nd.

28

P-51D-5-NA (NA.109) 44-13382 *February* of Lt James Brooks, 307th FS/31st FG, Fifteenth AAF
Brooks spent his first overseas assignment in Panama, before being sent to Italy in March 1944. Here, he claimed 13 aircraft destroyed in aerial combat, with three more probables and two damaged. Brooks resigned his commission in 1951 to become a test pilot for North American Aviation.

29

P-51D-5-NA (NA.109) 44-13464 of Maj Sam Brown, CO 307th FS/31st FG, Fifteenth AAF
Unusually, Maj Brown's P-51 lacked inboard yellow wing bands and tail stripes. He flew a tour in the Aleutians before joining the 31st FG. Claimed by some to be the 'best all-round fighter pilot' in the Fifteenth, Brown's tally of 15½ kills ranks him third behind Voll and Varnell.

30

P-51D-5-NA (NA.109) 44-13500 *Flying DUTCHMAN* of Capt Robert Goebel, 308th FS/31st FG, Fifteenth AAF
The sixth-highest scoring pilot of the 31st FG, Goebel claimed 11 kills during his 61-mission tour. His time in the frontline included a trip to Ploesti on 18 August 1944, during which he downed three Bf 109s. His P-51D continued to carry his old rank after his promotion to Captain – the 11 kill markings shown represent his final score, indicating the priorities of the man who wielded the paintbrush!

31

P-51D-5-NA (NA.109) 44-13494 *"MISS MIMI II"* of Capt Walter J Goehausen, Jr, 308th FS/31st FG, Fifteenth AAF
With ten kills, Goehausen was the sixth-highest scorer of the 31st FG. He made ace on 24 June 1944 over Ploesti, where the Group's pilots attained many kills.

32

P-51D-5-NA (NA.109) 44-13311 *OKaye* of Maj Leland P Molland, CO 308th FS/31st FG, Fifteenth AAF
Molland scored 6 of his 10½ kills while flying P-51s with the 31st FG. He started his career on Spitfires and stayed in the USAF postwar, being killed in action in Korea.

33

P-51D-15-NA (NA.109) 44-15459 *AMERICAN BEAUTY* of Capt John Voll, 308th FS/31st FG, Fifteenth AAF
John Voll was the third-highest scorer among all US P-51 pilots, and top Mustang ace in the MTO. His machine was named after a type of rose, a representation of which separated the two words of the name. Mustangs of the 31st FG initially had red spinners only, but a narrow red nose band was soon added. After the war Voll went back to civilian life as a teacher, but soon returned to duty and served in both Korea and Vietnam, retiring in 1969.

34

P-51D-25-NA (NA.124) 44-72777 of Maj Ralph J

'Doc' Watson, Ops Officer, 52nd FG, Fifteenth AAF

Watson took the last aircraft which he'd flown as CO of the 5th FS with him when he moved to become Group Ops Officer. Initially it retained the codes 'VF-V', but was soon re-coded 'MX-F'. He later served on the staff of the Fifteenth AAF's Mustang wing, serving as executive officer under Brig Yanis Taylor. In this appointment he flew a virtually unmarked P-51D, with no fuselage codes and with the colours of all four Fifteenth AAF Mustang Groups in a diamond on the tailfin, obscuring the serial. This aircraft depicted here later served with the Rhode Island and Californian ANGs, before being sold to Indonesia in 1972 as a Cavalier Mk 2 Mustang. It returned to the USA in 1979 and has since been restored to flying condition in 'Doc' Watson's markings.

35

P-51C-5-NT (NA.103) 42-103579 *Julie* of Lt Robert Curtis, 2nd FS/52nd FG, Fifteenth AAF

The 52nd FG used the same codes as the 4th FG in Britain; 'QP' for the 2nd, 'WD' for the 4th and 'VF' for the 5th. The 52nd FG had a black-edged yellow fuselage band as its identity marking, this treatment being repeated on its outer wing and tail bands. Flight commanders' P-51s in the 2nd FS wore a playing card insignia, often an ace – Curtis used a joker on his, a motif later employed on his similarly-coded yellow-tailed P-51D 44-14164.

36

P-51D-5-NA (NA.109) 44-13298 *"Marie"* of Capt Freddie F Ohr, 2nd FS/52nd FG, Fifteenth AAF

The 52nd FG replaced its original unit marking of a black-edged yellow band around the rear fuselage by extending the yellow back to cover the entire tail, including the horizontal tailplanes. Ohr's P-51 was unusual in wearing its individual letter in red – it was usually solid or outline black. The USAAF was more liberal in integrating oriental and native American pilots than it was in accepting Negroes. Thus, Lt Wah Kau Kong flew *Chinaman's Chance* with the 354th, and Lt Hiawatha Mohawk was a scoring pilot with the 325th, flying the *Blonde Squaw*. Ohr, with six kills (five in P-51s), was probably the only Korean ace in the USAAF.

37

P-51C-5-NT (NA.103) 42-103582 of Lt Calvin D Allen, Jr, 5th FS/52nd FG, Fifteenth AAF

This aircraft wears typical early 52nd FG markings, with the individual aircraft letter in yellow, outlined in black, on the tailfin, and with black-edged yellow bands around the rear fuselage and wingtips. A small red square behind the cockpit carries the flight designation, this P-51 being assigned to 'C' Flight. Believed to have been Duane Franklin's (seven P-51 kills) machine, this Mustang was also borrowed by Clarence Allen, Jr, for the mission during which he scored four of his seven victories.

38

P-51B-15-NA (NA.104) 43-24853 *Little Ambassador* of Lt James W Empey, 5th FS/52nd FG, Fifteenth AAF

Empey's P-51 was unusual among 52nd FG aircraft in being personalised, with name, nose art and kill tally. His 'girl' was a typical Varga pinup, and appeared behind the names of the pilot and groundcrew. Empey used 'VF-U' to score all of his five kills, downed in May and June of 1944.

39

P-51C-10-NT (NA.103) 42-103867 *SHIMMY III* of Lt Col Chester L Sluder, CO 325th FG, Fifteenth AAF

Although not an ace, with only two confirmed aerial victories, 'Chet' Sluder deserves inclusion in this book as one of the best group COs of the war. He used this aircraft as his mount when he led the first Shuttle mission of the war, Operation *Frantic Joe*, on 2 June 1944. His force of 64 P-51s landed at Piryatin, in Russia, and returned five days later after flying one mission from the Soviet base. *SHIMMY IV* was a similarly-marked P-51D which inspired the restoration of the aircraft in the USAF Museum. The first *SHIMMY* was an olive drab, checkertailed P-47, coded '52'. Sluder commanded the 325th from 1 April to 23 August 1944.

40

P-51D-5-NA (NA.109) 44-13483 *LITTLE STUD* of Col Robert L Baseler, CO 325th FG, Fifteenth AAF

After flying a 325th FG P-47 named *Big "STUD"* it was perhaps inevitable that six-victory ace (five on P-40s and one in a P-47) Baseler would name his P-51 replacement *LITTLE STUD*. This aircraft was later flown by Lt Col C H Beverley, who re-coded it '77' and re-named it *Belligerent Betts* – it was unusual in having a fine yellow line aft of the red nose band. The 325th FG adopted a yellow and black checkerboard tail as its marking, resulting in the 'Checkertail Clan' nickname. Initially the checkers were restricted to the tail, as seen here. Baseler later flew a natural metal P-47 (549355/'88') on a War Bond tour of the USA. This was also named *Big STUD* and painted in full 325th FG markings.

41

P-51D-5-NA (NA.109) 44-13299 *THISIZIT* of Capt Richard W Dunkin, 317th FS/325th FG, Fifteenth AAF

Nine-kill ace (one in P-40s and three in P-47s) Dunkin's *THISIZIT* combined an early limited-area checkertail with a red-outlined code. At war's end the 317th FS outlined its codes in red while the 319th used yellow.

42

P-51C-I-NT (NA.103) 42-103324 of Maj Herschel 'Herky' Green, CO 317th FS/325th FG, Fifteenth AAF

Top ace of the 325th FG, 'Herky' Green began his

combat career by taking off in his P-40 from the deck of USS *Ranger* on 19 January 1943, arriving in North Africa ready for combat soon afterwards. He subsequently flew the P-47, before the 325th converted to the P-51. Green stayed with the 325th for two-and-a-half years as pilot, squadron ops officer and CO. In 100 combat missions he downed 18 aircraft (including three in P-40s and 10 in P-47s) and destroyed ten more on the ground. His assigned aircraft were always coded '11'.

43
P-51D-5-NA (NA.109) 44-13440 *Ballzout II* of Lt Walter R Hinton, 317th FS/325th FG, Fifteenth AAF
Hinton flew two Mustangs named *Ballzout*. The first was a P-51C which he took on the first Shuttle mission to Russia. The second was this D-model, which wore Hinton's personal *'Spittin Kitten'* tiger badge. He scored several aerial kills, plus claimed hits on a Me 262 over Augsburg on 2 December 1944 while flying this machine in the 325th's first encounter with jets.

44 P-51B-15-NA (NA.104) 43-24877 *Penrod* of Capt Roy B Hogg, CO 318th FS/325th FG, Fifteenth AAF
The 325th's checkertail marking obscured the usual location of the aircraft serial number, although some, like six-kill ace Roy Hogg's *Penrod*, had the 'last three' repeated on the rear fuselage. This aircraft eventually returned to the UK and replaced Howard Hively's *The Deacon*.

45
P-51D-10-NA (NA.109) 44-14467 *MARY MAC* of Lt Gordon H McDaniel, 318th FS/325th FG, Fifteenth AAF
McDaniel was one of the rare breed to down five aircraft (all Fw 190s) during a single mission, achieving this feat on 14 March 1945. Unusually for a P-51 from the 325th, his *MARY MAC* had red wingtips. It also displays the later style increased-area checkertail, which covered the entire rear fuselage and tail unit. He inherited the P-51 from Jim Toner, CO of the 318th, who had coded it '00'.

46
P-51D-20-NA 44-63512 *SHU SHU* of Maj Norman L McDonald, CO 318th FS/325th FG, Fifteenth AAF
McDonald flew two tours, the first in Spitfires with the 52nd FG. He returned to operations as CO of the 318th FS, and brought his total missions to 249 by VE-Day. McDonald scored four victories while with the 325th, bringing his total to 11$\frac{1}{2}$, plus five probables and seven damaged. His P-51 wore no kill markings until near the end of the conflict.

47
P-51B-15-NA (NA.104) 43-24857 *Dorothy-II* of Capt Robert M Barkey, 319th FS/325th FG, Fifteenth AAF
Barkey completed 53 combat missions with the 325th, 45 in a P-47 named *Thunderbolt Lad* after his young son. He flew another eight sorties in *Dorothy-II*, named after his wife. Barkey downed five aircraft (four in P-47s), plus a probable.

48
P-51B/C *TOPPER III* of Capt Ed Toppins, 99th FS/332nd FG, Fifteenth AAF
Most 332nd FG Mustangs had names or nose art, and this was usually repeated on both sides of the aircraft. The Group's four units all had red tails, and spinners, with nose bands and trim tabs providing individual squadron markings. Many aircraft also had red wingtips. This aircraft was flown by Capt Ed Toppins, who scored four victories, and wore his kill markings below the windscreen. The blue and white checkerboard nose marking originally applied to 99th FS P-51s was later replaced by a plain blue nose band. As the fourth unit in its original Group, and then of the 332nd, the 99th FS wore A-prefixed codes, with the two-digit number broken by the star and bar on the fuselage. Codes ran from 'A0-0' to 'A3-9'.

49
P-51D-15-NA (NA.109) 44-15569 *BUNNIE* of Capt Roscoe C Brown, CO 100th FS/332nd FG, Fifteenth AAF
This P-51D has often been incorrectly assigned to Col Benjamin Davis, CO of the 332nd FG, and was the aircraft used for a series of publicity photos ostensibly showing the commanders of the four Fifteenth AAF Mustang groups. Brown had stood in for Davis on this occasion, however, since Davis had little patience with such publicity stunts, and was not confident about his own formation flying skills. The photo flight was undertaken twice, and between the first and second missions, Brown's P-51 received its *Bunnie* name (Brown's daughter). Brown scored two kills, one against an Me 262. The 100th FS used a red nose-band, sometimes with a blaze, and had black trim-tabs. The red undercarriage doors were non-standard, and appeared only on HQ aircraft. Red-outlined codes became more common as the war neared its end, and the red area on the tail was increased, sweeping up from the rudder to a point forward of the aerial on the spine. 100th FS P-51s wore codes running from '00' to '39'.

50
P-51C-5-NT (NA.103) *Miss-Pelt* of Lt Clarence 'Lucky' Lester, 100th FS/332nd FG, Fifteenth AAF
Lester gained fame by becoming the first Negro pilot to down three aircraft in a single mission. He flew at least two similarly-marked P-51Bs, the other machine having *Miss-Pelt* applied in red block letters, and with no candy striping on the antenna above the cockpit – it also had square, non-angled swastikas as kill markings. This aircraft

was unusual in that it lacked yellow theatre bands on the underside of the wings.

51

P-51D *Creamer's Dream* of Lt Charles White, 301st FS/332nd FG, Fifteenth AAF

The Mustangs of the 301st FS used white trim-tabs as their unit marking, with red nose-bands. White was one of the first 332nd pilots to receive a P-51D – joining the unit as a replacement pilot he had received a war-weary P-51C, and his complaints about its unreliability led his CO to allocate him one of the first P-51Ds. White painted a nude on both sides of the fuselage, with an aft view to port, and a full-frontal to starboard! 301st FS Mustangs wore codes running from '40' to '69'.

52

P-51C-10-NT (NA.111) *"INA The MACON BELLE"* of Lt Lee 'Buddy' Archer, 302nd FS/332nd FG, Fifteenth AAF

Originally named *"The MACON BELLE"*, Archer's squadron-mates added the name *"Ina"* when they discovered the name of Archer's sweetheart. Archer and Wendell Pruitt's deadly partnership led to their nickname of the 'Gruesome Twosome', and since both were 'sophisticated city boys from Northern towns', their aircraft each received an identical ironic caricature, showing a 'Hep Cat' in a 'Zoot Suit'. The aircraft had a yellow band around each wing in the position normally associated with P-51As and A-36s, although red wingtips and red-outlined codes were also worn. Pruitt flew the similarly-marked *Alice-Jo*, coded '73'. Archer scored more than five kills, and he was thus probably the only Negro ace, though he is reluctant to cause a fuss today, so long after the war. The 301st FS's Mustangs wore codes running from '70' to '99'.

53

P-51D *"Little Freddie"* of Lt Freddie Hutchins, 302nd FS/332nd FG, Fifteenth AAF

Most 302nd P-51s had red and yellow striped noses, though some did not have the red stripes applied. Unusually, Hutchins' P-51 did not have red-outlined codes or outboard theatre identification bands. Yellow trim tabs were used by the 302nd as a unit identification marking, along with the candy-striped noses. The 302nd FS was the most successful of the four Negro units.

54

Mustang Mk III FZ152 of Wg Cdr Stanislaw Skalski, OC No 133 Wg, RAF

Like their USAAF group commander counterparts, RAF wing commanders often used their own initials in lieu of unit codes. This D-Day striped Mk III wears the 'SS' codes of Stanislaw Skalski, together with his 21 kills. Upper surface stripes were overpainted from September, except on the Allison-engined low-level Mk I/IAs, which never had them.

55

Mustang Mk III FB201 of Flg Off B M Vassiliades, No 19 Sqn, RAF

With six of his nine kills scored in the Mk III, Vassiliades was one of the top RAF Mustang aces. He used this Mk III (as did his CO, Sqn Ldr Peter Hearne, with five Mustang kills) to score two of his victories. RAF Mustangs gained white spinners and nose bands, and white bands across their fins, tailplanes and wings during December 1943 to bring them into line with USAAF P-51s. The fin band was soon removed, and most tailplane bands had gone by March 1944, but the other markings remained. Wing bands were displaced by D-Day stripes, but white noses lasted longer.

56

Mustang Mk III FZ120 of Sqn Ldr Derrick Westenra, OC No 65 Sqn, RAF

Westenra scored 2$\frac{1}{3}$ Mustang victories out of a final tally of 8, and 3 shared. Together with No 19 Sqn, No 65 were among the RAF's most successful Mk III operators, taking advantage of the type's long-range to mount sweeps and escorts to Scandinavia, often accompanying Coastal Command aircraft. Mustangs started to have their camouflage removed following an order dated 8 March 1945. By VE-Day most Mustangs remained camouflaged, however, although a significant number of Mk IVs were in natural metal finish.

57

Mustang Mk III FB309 of Flt Lt Raymond V Hearn, No 112 Sqn, RAF

Hearn flew two tours with No 112 Sqn on Kittyhawks and Mustangs. He is best remembered as the cool, but indomitable, commander of 'B' Flight, and used the individual letter 'Q' on his aircraft. He downed a Ju 88 in this machine on 9 September 1944, even though only one of his four guns was working. He was killed on what was to have been his last sortie on 18 February 1945, his aircraft (Mustang Mk IV KH820/'Q') exploding after being hit by flak. The letter 'Q' was not used again by No 112 Sqn as a mark of respect.

58

Mustang Mk III FZ149 of Flt Sgt W Nowoczyn, No 306 *Torunski* Sqn, RAF

Nowoczyn was one of no less than 24 *Diver* aces, scoring exactly five kills. On 17 August, units engaged in anti-*Diver* operations were ordered to remove the yellow leading edge stripes from their wings, although this order was not universally obeyed, and many Mustangs had the stripes re-applied when they returned to fighter duties, although such re-applied stripes often extended only as far inboard as the outer gun port. Many of the Mk IIIs combating V1s were waxed and polished in order to squeeze the last few knots of performance from them.

59

Mustang Mk III FB387of Sqn Ldr Eugeniusz Horbaczewski, No 315 *Deblinski* Sqn, RAF

The Poles often applied squadron markings to their aircraft, and also seemed more likely to add kill and mission markings. This aircraft was flown by Sqn Ldr Horbaczewski, whose $5^1/2$ Mustang victories gave him a total of $16^1/2$ kills. Flying Mk IIIs for only a short time, he scored his first kill in the aircraft on 12 June 1944, immediately after which he landed to pick up a downed pilot. On 18 August Horbaczewski claimed his last score – a trio of Fw 190s – but failed to return from the mission.

60

Mustang Mk I AG470 of Flg Off Hollis Hills, No 414 Sqn, RCAF

The Mustang Mk Is were delivered in dark green and dark earth camouflage with sky lower surfaces. They soon received sky spinners and fuselage bands in service, and from July 1942 also gained type recognition markings consisting of a yellow leading edge and 12-inch wide yellow chordwise wing bands which were added to prevent confusion with the Bf 109. By the time Hills scored his historic kill on 19 August 1942, dark earth had given way to dark grey, and the sky undersides had been replaced with medium sea grey, this change in colour scheme also being ordered on 1 July 1942. The chordwise bands were removed from December 1942, but many aircraft retained them for much longer. Most No 414 Sqn Mustangs wore a small maple leaf on the nose, together with a small horse's head that served as an unofficial unit badge.

FIGURE PLATES

1

Lt Wendell O Pruitt of the 302nd FS/332nd FG is seen in mid-1944 wearing A-9 trousers, paired with a B-15 flying jacket. Over his jacket is a standard-issue B-3 life preserver, whilst Pruitt wears an RAF C Type helmet on his head, fitted with B-8 goggles and A-10 oxygen mask. Stuffed in the thigh pocket of his A-9 trousers are a pair of highly-prized 1941-pattern RAF flying gloves, preferred bymany USAAF fighter pilots over the US issue B-3s. Finally, Pruitt is wearing standard-issue QMC boots.

2

Lt Lee 'Buddy' Archer is seen here in flying kit quite dissimilar to Pruitt. Although he is wearing similar QMC boots and A-9 trousers (note that he has removed the thigh pocket and had a see-through zippered map panel fitted in its place), Archer's jacket takes the form of a leather A-2. Over this is worn an RAF 1941 issue Mark I 'Mae West', paired with British gloves from the same year. His helmet is also RAF issue, being a Type D tropical, although his B-7 goggles are standard issue USAAF pattern. Finally, Archer's personal equipment is completed with the addition of an A-10 oxygen mask.

3

Lt Col Glenn T Eagleston, CO of the 353rd FS and top scoring ace of the 354th FG. He is seen here in the spring of 1945 wearing his beige 'pinks' (with matching tie) and standard issue GI shoes, whilst his 'crush' cap crown and shirt have been cut in non-standard dark brown material adopted by US officers late in the war – the standard issue shade for such items was olive drab. On the collar of Eagleston's shirt is his rank badge, whilst his 'wings' are pinned to his chest above the left breast pocket. On his sleeve is a Ninth AAF patch, and he has an A-2 over his shoulder, to which is attached a whistle. Finally, Eagleston is carrying an RAF issue Type C helmet, paired with ubiquitous B-7 goggles.

4

Wearing a lightweight 'Suit, Summer, Flying', AN-S-31A over his 'pinks', Lt Bruce W Carr of the 353rd FS/354th FG is seen in mid-April 1945. Around his waist is a B-3 life preserver, below which is a 1936-pattern pistol belt supporting a 1911A1 .45 in Colt. Over Carr's shoulder, attached to the S-1 harness, is the B-2 survival pack and AN-6510 parachute. Completing his uniform is the '50-mission crush' cap.

5

Standing out in his RAF battledress 'blues', Flg Off Hollis H Hills hails from No 414 Sqn, RCAF, in August 1942. Like later Mustang pilots of the USAAF, he is wearing a Mark I 'Mae West', Type B flying helmet, Mark IV goggles and Type D oxygen mask. Hollis is carrying civilian-pattern sheepskin gloves, and note the unique 'CANADA/USA' shoulder flash.

6

A member of the 363rd FG, Maj Robert C McWherter is wearing A-6A single strap winter-issue boots, with his olive drab service trousers tucked into them. A B-15 jacket adorned with a Ninth AAF patch and major's rank tabs covers his top half, beneath which he is wearing a white scarf. A B-3 life preserver rests on the B-15, and like most other AAF fighter pilots in the ETO, McWherter is wearing an RAF issue Type C helmet. B-8 goggles are attached to his headgear, as is an A-10 mask. However, unlike his brethren, he has chosen to wear goatskin A-10 gloves, lined with camel hair.

INDEX

References to illustrations are shown in **bold**. Colour Plates are prefixed 'pl.' and Figure Plates 'fig.pl.', with page and caption locators in brackets.